THE LEADERSHIP OF ABRAHAM LINCOLN

PROBLEMS IN AMERICAN HISTORY

EDITOR

LOREN BARITZ

State University of New York, Albany

THE LEADERSHIP OF ABRAHAM LINCOLN
Don E. Fehrenbacher

THE AMERICAN CONSTITUTION
Paul Goodman

THE AMERICAN REVOLUTION
Richard J. Hooker

AMERICA IN THE COLD WAR
Walter LaFeber

ORIGINS OF THE COLD WAR, 1941–1947
Walter LaFeber

AMERICAN IMPERIALISM IN 1898
Richard H. Miller

TENSIONS IN AMERICAN PURITANISM
Richard Reinitz

THE GREAT AWAKENING
Darrett B. Rutman

WORLD WAR I AT HOME
David F. Trask

THE CRITICAL YEARS,
AMERICAN FOREIGN POLICY, 1793–1825
Patrick C. T. White

THE LEADERSHIP OF ABRAHAM LINCOLN

DON E. FEHRENBACHER

Professor of History
Stanford University

John Wiley & Sons, Inc.

New York • *London* • *Sydney* • *Toronto*

SERIES PREFACE

This series is an introduction to the most important problems in the writing and study of American history. Some of these problems have been the subject of debate and argument for a long time, although others only recently have been recognized as controversial. However, in every case, the student will find a vital topic, an understanding of which will deepen his knowledge of social change in America.

The scholars who introduce and edit the books in this series are teaching historians who have written history in the same general area as their individual books. Many of them are leading scholars in their fields, and all have done important work in the collective search for better historical understanding.

Because of the talent and the specialized knowledge of the individual editors, a rigid editorial format has not been imposed on them. For example, some of the editors believe that primary source material is necessary to their subjects. Some believe that their material should be arranged to show conflicting interpretations. Others have decided to use the selected materials as evidence for their own interpretations. The individual editors have been given the freedom to handle their books in the way that their own experience and knowledge indicate is best. The overall result is a series built up from the individual decisions of working scholars in the various fields, rather than one that conforms to a uniform editorial decision.

A common goal (rather than a shared technique) is the bridge of this series. There is always the desire to bring the reader as close to these problems as possible. One result of this objective is an emphasis on the nature and consequences of problems and events, with a de-emphasis of the more purely historiographical issues. The goal is to involve the student in the reality of crisis, the inevitability of ambiguity, and the excitement of finding a way through the historical maze.

Above all, this series is designed to show students how experienced historians read and reason. Although health is not contagious, intellectual engagement may be. If we show students something significant in a phrase or a passage that they otherwise may have missed, we will have accomplished part of our objective. When students see something that passed us by, then the process will have been made whole. This active and mutual involvement of editor and reader with a significant human problem will rescue the study of history from the smell and feel of dust.

Loren Baritz

CONTENTS

THE LEADERSHIP OF ABRAHAM LINCOLN

INTRODUCTION

The historical Lincoln can never be separated completely from the Lincoln legend or disentangled from the tradition of the Civil War, which is itself a mixture of history and legend. The drama of his death, for instance, inevitably colors the story of his life, and the image of the Great Emancipator persists in spite of doubts about its accuracy. Lincoln's rise from obscurity, his attractive personal qualities, and the lean eloquence of his language have all contributed to placing him first in the affections of the American people. But the enduring stature of the man is also an indication of the unique place that the Civil War occupies in the nation's historical consciousness. Furthermore, Lincoln's career from 1854 until his death closely corresponded to the general sweep and perhaps inexorable logic of history. For this reason, it is exceedingly difficult to measure the weight of his presence on the scene—to determine how much of a difference he made. No doubt his influence has often been exaggerated, but few historians would accept at face value Lincoln's own assertion: "I claim not to have controlled events, but confess plainly that events have controlled me."

The vitality of the Lincoln tradition must be attributed in no small part to the continuing relevance of its major themes. The problem of the Negro's place in American life is by far the most obvious and most important connection between Lincoln's generation and our own, but there are others. What are the limits of majority rule and minority rights? Where is the boundary between dissent and disloyalty? How should a conflict between law and conscience be resolved? Is a polity that can be saved only by force worth saving at all? Can armed revolution ever be justi-

1

fied in a democratic society? Is compromise always preferable to war? What is the proper relationship between civil and military authority? Is military conscription compatible with the ideal of liberty? Can the Supreme Court be permitted to determine public policy without a consequent erosion of the democratic process? Is the president vested with inherent powers sufficient to meet any emergency that may arise? These questions that confronted Lincoln and his contemporaries have lost none of their urgency a century later.

Because of its continuing relevance, the study of the Civil War era is often affected by current controversy and may be used for polemical purposes. The past can be illumined with new meaning and at the same time be seriously distorted by the imperatives of the present. Lincoln has been obscured not only by his own legend and by the Civil War tradition that envelops him, but also by a tendency to enlist him in the causes, confront him with the problems, measure him by the standards, and see him through the eyes of ages other than his own.

It is difficult to resense the temper and perspective of Lincoln's generation, whose values were rooted in the preindustrial America of its youth and whose vision of the future, still essentially optimistic, accented individual initiative far more than social action. The very idea of social reform was of recent origin, and Lincoln could not be numbered among its votaries. As Lord Charnwood observed, "He accepted the institutions to which he was born, and he enjoyed them." It could easily have been Lincoln, instead of Henry David Thoreau, who wrote: "I came into this world, not chiefly to make this a good place to live in, but to live in it, be it good or bad."

To be accurate, however, Charnwood's statement must be qualified in one important respect. Lincoln regarded slavery as a "vast moral evil." He "accepted" the institution only in the sense that he acknowledged its legal status and his own inability to see any way of uprooting it in the near future. Possessing little of our modern zeal for crusading as a life style, Lincoln nevertheless became involved in the crusade against slavery. So, for that matter, did Thoreau, but it was Lincoln who eventually presided over the greatest single reform in American history. The opportunity to play such a role came to him because the somewhat devious course of his attack on slavery was a direct route to political power.

Because he was a politician, the purpose of gaining and retaining power was seldom far from Lincoln's thoughts. It blended with his other purposes and influenced most of his actions not only before but after he became president. That it was the dominant and even sole purpose of his career has sometimes been asserted, but this cynical view is probably as far from the truth as the sentimental image of a man who entered politics only in order to perform noble deeds. For example, there are two ways of describing Lincoln's reaction to the Kansas-Nebraska Bill in 1854. One is that his strong feeling against the extension of slavery drew him back into active politics; the other, that he saw in the new slavery controversy a splendid opportunity for his own political advancement. Either explanation by itself is inadequate and misleading, but a combination of the two comes close to the mark. Moral commitment *and* personal ambition propelled Lincoln in the same direction.

Lincoln's struggle for power did not end with his election to the presidency but merely entered a new and more complex phase. It now became a struggle to establish and maintain control, to exert his own will against the force of other powerful wills. Only a few weeks after his inauguration, he had to turn aside the offer of a Cabinet member virtually to take over the duties of the presidency. He had to deal with a congressional committee that wanted to direct military operations and with various generals who wanted to make political policy. Most important, without vacating his position as party leader, he had to secure and retain bipartisan support for prosecution of the war. Thus, he justified emancipation as a military necessity not only for constitutional reasons but in an effort to placate many Northerners who were willing to fight for preservation of the Union but not for the abolition of slavery. With much insight, James Russell Lowell compared Lincoln to a man taking "a rather shackly raft through the rapids, making fast the unrulier logs as he could snatch opportunity." The most statesmanlike steering would have been in vain without the politician's success in holding the craft together.

Although he never ceased to be a politician, Lincoln's partisanship in later years lacked the fervor of his youthful devotion to Whiggery. Contrary to a widely accepted notion, he made the transition from Whig to Republican with no great reluctance and at the earliest appropriate time. In 1864, he readily gave up the Republican label to seek reelection as the nominee of the "Union Party," with a War Democrat as his running-mate. As president, Lincoln dispensed patronage in the orthodox partisan fashion, but on the military side, he did not hesitate to install a Democrat, Edwin M. Stanton, as secretary of war, and he resisted pressure for restricting army command to loyal Republicans. After 1854, he tended increasingly to regard party politics as a means rather than an end.

The pattern of Lincoln's political career in the 1850's is fairly simple because he was inspired by just two closely-related purposes—winning election to office and preventing the extension of slavery. His presidential years, of course, are something else again. The exercise of power required more political skill and versatility than the winning of office. The progress of emancipation, with all of its racial implications and urgent practical problems, added much complexity to the old issue of slavery. Most important, when civil war mushroomed out of the sectional crisis, the problem of slavery was subordinated to the task of saving the Union without losing any of its explosive force. The pattern of interrelated purposes now became more intricate and less congruous. Any action taken on the slavery front, for instance, had to be weighed for its probable effect on the military and political fronts. This did not mean discounting the moral issue of slavery but rationalizing it in the existing circumstances. Total emancipation, after all, depended upon winning the war, which in turn depended upon maintaining a concerted will to fight.

The study of Lincoln's leadership is therefore by no means a simple undertaking, but it requires concentration on just a few major themes: slavery and the Negro, the Union and the war to preserve it, and the struggle for political power. To other matters, such as the conduct of foreign relations and the enactment of even highly important domestic legislation, the president rarely gave more than perfunctory attention. It is, in fact, surprising to find this former Whig only mildly interested in the issues that had once animated his party—issues like the tariff, banking, public lands, and internal improvements. But Lincoln had always been one to confine his intellectual energies within a narrow range. He had "the gift of selectivity," according to one scholar. "His whole genius was for concentration," writes another. Many subjects deserving inclusion in a history of Lincoln's administration are of little use in exploring the nature of his leadership.

Accordingly, the readings offered in this book are limited to the primary themes of his presidential career and the principal questions raised by historical scholarship. For the most part, these questions fall into three categories: What were Lincoln's motives and intentions? How successful and how decisive were his efforts? And how fortunate or unfortunate were the consequences? The first category is the least important of the three for historians but lies at the very heart of the biographer's task. Meaningful answers to questions of this kind are almost unavoidably speculative in some degree. Such is the case, for example, with the various explanations of why Lincoln stood fast against compromise during the secession winter of 1860–1861. The second category undoubtedly lends itself most readily to systematic investigation and objective verification. Yet it has produced its full share of scholarly controversies and dubious conclusions. Lincoln has been labeled both a success and a failure in his relations with the Radical Republicans, as well as in his direction of military affairs. The part that he played in the creation of the Republican party is often underestimated, while the weight of his responsibility for the failure of compromise in 1861 is probably exaggerated. Questions in the third category call for the value judgments that are usually responsive not only to the historical data but also to the historian's own temperament and social outlook. The lines of inquiry shift with the changing times, and new questions, as well as new answers to old questions, emerge from the continual quest for a relevant past. Until recently, for instance, the historical context of Lincoln studies has been a conflict between white men over the institution of slavery, with the Negro playing a more or less passive role. But the new black history, which emphasizes the Negro's own struggle for freedom and treats slavery as an aspect of racism, is putting the Civil War and Lincoln's leadership in a different perspective.

To be complete, a study of leadership should probably take some account of things not done, but the limits of relevance and possibility are hard to set. After the election of 1860, Lincoln might have made a strong effort to reassure the Southern people, and the situation seemed to call for it. His considered refusal to act was the equivalent of an action taken and subject to the same kind of analysis. At the other extreme, there is little historical meaning in the indisputable fact that the Lincoln administration did not eliminate racial discrimination in education or establish a social security program. Within the bounds of relevance and possibility, perhaps Lincoln's greatest sin of omission was that, in his eagerness to reconstruct the Union, he gave too little consideration to the pressing needs of the freedmen and the postwar problem of racial readjustment. Remembering that he died just a few days after Appomattox, one can understand and even excuse his inadvertence, but the consequences were none the less unfortunate.

Supplementing the list of things not done is the record of efforts made in vain. Conspicuous examples are Lincoln's plans for gradual, compensated emancipation and for colonization of free Negroes abroad. These proposals reveal much about Lincoln's thought and even more about the society to which he was suiting his thought. They confirm his general pessimism about racial attitudes in nineteenth-century America. The very recommendations were in themselves actions of a limited sort, having effects that may not have been inconsequential. Yet such abortive efforts seldom compare in significance with purposes actually achieved and plans converted into action.

At the center of attention in any evaluation of leadership are those courses of action that have been deliberately chosen from among alternatives, that are pursued to successful conclusions, and that have decisive effects. The Emancipation Proclamation is the obvious case in point. It is by examining and weighing these elements of choice, accomplishment, and consequence that one can estimate the extent to which the times made the man and the man shaped his times.

PART ONE

Lincoln and the Coming of the Civil War

Lincoln and the Coming of the Civil War

Either the *opponents* of slavery will arrest the further spread of it, and place it where the public mind shall rest in the belief that it is in course of ultimate extinction; or its *advocates* will push it forward till it shall become alike lawful in *all* the States, *old* as well as *new—North* as well as *South*.

LINCOLN, HOUSE-DIVIDED SPEECH, JUNE 16, 1858

Never forget that we have before us this whole matter of the right or wrong of slavery in this Union, though the immediate question is as to its spreading out into new Territories and States.

LINCOLN, SPEECH AT CHICAGO, MARCH 1, 1859

It was with the deepest regret that the Executive found the duty of employing the war-power, in defence of the government, forced upon him. He could but perform this duty, or surrender the existence of the government. No compromise by public servants could, in this case, be a cure; not that compromises are not often proper, but that no popular government can long survive a marked precedent, that those who carry an election can only save the government from immediate destruction by giving up the main point upon which the people gave the election.

LINCOLN, MESSAGE TO CONGRESS, JULY 4, 1861

To say that Lincoln meant that the first shot would be fired by the other side *if a first shot was fired,* is by no means the equivalent of saying that he deliberately maneuvered to have the shot fired. This distinction is fundamental.

J. G. RANDALL, 1940

Possessing no realistic formula for achieving the peaceful elimination of slavery against the South's determination to maintain it, neither Lincoln nor any other antislavery politician of the North could present to the nation any genuine alternative but civil war to indefinite coexistence with slavery.

NORMAN A. GRAEBNER, 1961

To what extent was Abraham Lincoln personally responsible for the coming of the Civil War? Discussion of this question falls into three distinct categories: (1) his part in shaping the character of the Republican party and precipitating the secession movement; (2) his conduct during the crucial months between his election and inauguration; (3) his strategy in the Fort Sumter crisis. All three of these subjects are treated in the selections that follow. T. Harry Williams, a major figure in Civil War historiography, does not defend the Republican stand on slavery but instead endeavors to explain how reasonable men of the time could take such a stand. His purpose is to see things as Lincoln saw them in the 1850's. Williams is a Midwesterner who became a Louisianan early in his professional career. Harold S. Schultz, in contrast, is a New Englander transplanted from the upper South. According to Schultz, Republican insistence upon prohibition of slavery in the territories was unrealistic and harmful; furthermore, Lincoln erred grievously, as president-elect, in refusing to endorse proposals for compromise. His argument reflects the influence of the revisionist or it-could-and-should-have-been-averted school of Civil War scholarship. The noted historian Allan Nevins, in his four imposing volumes on the coming of the Civil War, offered an eclectic interpretation and found himself criticized as both too pro-Northern and too pro-Southern. But in the passages analyzing Lincoln's rejection of compromise, his sympathies are clearly with the man who said *No*. Richard N. Current, in recent years probably the ranking Lincoln specialist among professional historians, is but one of several able scholars who have studied the Fort Sumter crisis in detail. In the selection reprinted here, he presents a fair summary and a persuasive refutation of the "Ramsdell thesis" that Lincoln deliberately maneuvered the Confederates into firing the first shot.

1   *T. Harry Williams*
The Issue that Could Not Be Put Off

More than any Republican, Lincoln stressed that slavery was on the march, that it was aggressively reaching out into new areas: the territories and possibly the free states themselves. He did not say positively that this thrust was the result of a deliberate plan, of an organized movement, but he hinted strongly at the possibility. We know today that there was no purposeful all-southern effort to extend slavery. Some Southerners, it is true, belligerently demanded *Lebensraum* for slavery, even at the expense of a foreign war to annex regions in Latin America. But most Southerners would have preferred to let the question of actual expansion lie dormant. They might talk firmly and bravely, especially for northern consumption, about the right to take their slave property into the territories, but they were contending for an abstraction. In private or in cooler moments they would have admitted that only a fraction of the territories might conceivably be won for slavery. The South, in some of the crises of the 1850's, notably in the furor surrounding the Kansas-Nebraska

SOURCE. T. Harry Williams, "The Causes of the Civil War," in O. Fritiof Ander, ed., *Lincoln Images: Augustana College Centennial Essays* (Rock Island, Illinois: Augustana Library Publications, 1960), pp. 35–39. Reprinted by permission of the publisher and the author.

Act, was not the aggressor, but permitted itself to be jockeyed into a position of apparent aggression by a few extremist politicians, most of them from the border states.

Lincoln then, was wrong in thinking that slavery was moving on to new conquests, and especially wrong in suspecting that there was some kind of organized scheme to push it into new areas. But the conclusions that many historians have drawn from this judgment need analysis. These conclusions are, whether or not they were so bluntly stated, that Lincoln and other Republicans were, if not fools, certainly not very perceptive observers, or that they were, if not charlatans, designing politicians deliberately riding a false issue into office. The most charitable interpretation to be put upon the course of the Republicans is that they did not realize what they were doing, that they were carelessly playing with fire. Now if we know anything, it is that Abraham Lincoln was not a fool. And we know, too, that while Lincoln was a politician, superbly skilled and certainly ambitious, he was one with a high degree of principle. To say that he did not understand what was happening or that he understood and did not consider the results simply does not make sense. We must look for another explanation.

We will never comprehend the events of the 1850's if we insist on looking at them through our eyes. That decade, like every other period, is a living, vibrant page of history, and while we may admit that sometimes men act from motives of which they are unaware, still we must try to see the motives they thought they had. How, then, did things appear to Lincoln and other Republicans in those years? They saw a sequence of happenings that disturbed them, and they came to a conclusion, which if not inevitable, was certainly natural for them to reach. The Compromise of 1850, coming after a dangerous crisis, had seemed to settle finally the sectional controversy. Then four years later the Kansas-Nebraska Act, apparently but not actually an expression of southern aggression, *seemed* to open new territory to slavery. Then the Dred Scott decision was announced, hitting the Republicans like a bombshell. The broad tenor of the decision is well-known, but the implications in some of the opinions have not been adequately analyzed and it was these implications that troubled the Republicans and notably Lincoln. It was not just that the Supreme Court said Congress could not exclude slavery from the territories, bad as that was. Chief Justice Taney and Justice Nelson, whether or not they meant to, seemed to go much farther. They said that the right to property in slaves was "expressly affirmed" in the Constitution. That is, slavery had a special and specific sanctity not attached to other forms of property.

This was the part of the decision that aroused Lincoln, that led him to charge that there was a deliberate plan to extend slavery. For if slavery was expressly protected by the Constitution, could a state, even a state where it did not exist, bar it? Would not some future decision open all the states to slavery? We think that Lincoln read more into the decision than was there, but was his reaction without reason? One other feature of the case deserves notice. Professor Harry Jaffa has said that the Dred Scott decision was a summons to the Republican party to disband. If it was not quite that, it was a judicial declaration that the platform of a major party was unconstitutional. On several occasions in our history the Supreme Court has placed itself in a position where it seemed to be thwarting the will of a large proportion of the people, but seldom if ever has it done so as starkly as in 1857. Is it then so surprising that Lincoln thought there was something queer afoot? Or that he denounced the decision as a blow at popular government? . . .

By the 1850's the controversy over slavery had reached a point where some kind of settlement had to be made. The issue was too big, too dangerous to be put off. Either the majority North had to be satisfied that a way would be found to get rid of slavery, preferably a way satisfactory to the South, or the North had to admit that slavery was a permanent institution on the American scene and stop attacking it. The latter probability was so unlikely that it may be dismissed. There remained the possibility that the North and the South could devise some solution acceptable to both. This was exactly what Lincoln was trying to do when he proposed his plan to bring about the destruction of slavery by excluding it from the territories. If slavery was penned up in the South, he thought, it would eventually disappear. His policy would, he liked to say, place slavery in such a condition as to bring about its ultimate extinction. Lincoln always stressed

the word ultimate in discussing the end of slavery. The process
he recommended would take years to complete; it was a kind of
patient emancipation. But it was, and this is sometimes forgotten
by critics, a fundamental solution. Finally there would be no
slavery in America. Lincoln hoped that his plan would satisfy
both sections.

Lincoln's solution was not adopted, nor was any plan to resolve
the crisis put in motion. The South was not prepared to offer
a plan of its own that involved any yielding on the question of
race relationships. Professor Allan Nevins has criticized southern leaders for not nerving their people to pay the necessary
price of race adjustment. But even if the leaders had favored
some kind of compromise, they would not have dared to propose
it—for the simple reason that the people would not hear of it.
Perhaps the greatest tragedy of the sectional controversy is that
the South could not proffer a solution. Of northern opinion we
cannot speak with much certainty. We do not know if the North
would have waited patiently for the South to change its attitude
or if the North would have been satisfied with some gradual plan
like Lincoln's; shortly the whole question would become aca-
demic. Humans cannot always control history, and when they do
not history may determine its own course. By 1860 the situation
was well out of the power of the American people to decide. Then
only one resolution was possible. As Lincoln aptly put it: "And
the war came."

2   *Harold S. Schultz*
           Partisan or Patriot?

It is impossible to write of Lincoln, America's greatest symbol
of patriotism, without being hackneyed. Lincoln, the man who

SOURCE. Harold S. Schultz, "Lincoln: Partisan or Patriot?" in *The Social
Studies*, LIV (1963) , pp. 63–68. Reprinted by permission of the publisher
and the author.

saved the Union, towers above Lincoln the Great Emancipator, higher than the Liberal Statesman, higher than the earthy hero of folksy Democracy. Lincoln the Union-Saver is, however, no fictional creation of a posterity that unconsciously uses the hero as an instrument to promote national solidarity and patriotism. The record of what the man said throughout his career and what he did in the presidency sustains popular opinion as to his patriotism.

In Lincoln's writings are to be found, abundantly expressed, his reverential awe and appreciation for the founders of the republic. Over and over again he praised the superior virtues of American institutions; repeatedly he sought to articulate what he felt to be the unique American spirit. At the very highest level in his scale of political values was preservation of the American Union. The seeking after local or sectional interests, legitimate to a degree, must never be permitted to rise above national interests. The pursuit of an ideal, such as abolition of slavery, though obligatory as a moral imperative, must never be carried to the point of jeopardizing the Union. Although Lincoln reprimanded Douglas for declining to denounce the immorality of slavery, he at no time in his life took the position that slavery was as great an evil as disunion. When Lincoln made the decision to issue the Emancipation Proclamation he tried to make clear that the Union was still the touchstone of all his policies. In a public letter of August 22, 1862, addressed to Horace Greeley, he said: "My paramount object in this struggle *is* to save the Union, and is *not* either to save or destroy Slavery. If I could save the Union without freeing *any* slave, I would do it; and if I could save it by freeing *all* the slaves, I would do it; and if I could do it by freeing some and leaving others alone, I would also do that. What I do about Slavery and the colored race, I do because I believe it helps to save this Union; and what I forbear, I forbear because I do *not* believe it would help to save the Union."

Lincoln, of course, it must be said in all fairness, never saw preservation of national unity as an alternative that excluded other cherished values. The American Union for him was the vehicle for demonstrating the blessings of liberty and democracy to the world: national disintegration would be synonymous with the destruction of liberty and democracy. This he explained in his message to Congress, July 4, 1861; this he stated most eloquently in the address at Gettysburg, November 19, 1863.

As President, Lincoln did more than compose fine phrases about democracy, liberty, and the Union. He worked incessantly to win the war. He patiently managed a cabinet of party leaders who represented all the diverse segments of the Republican Party and which included four disappointed rivals for the nomination of 1860. Calmly, and with fortitude, he encountered the partisan attacks of the Democratic opposition in Congress and in the Northern press. Nor was he ever free from attacks by the more radical members of his own party who criticized his conduct of the war, his reluctance to emancipate the slaves, and his leniency toward Confederate states reconquered by the Union armies. Conscientiously he studied the daily reports from the battlefields or visited the armies in northern Virginia to learn for himself how the war was progressing. In selecting the top generals, ability and loyalty to the Union were his only criteria; personal shortcomings, party allegiance, or ideological beliefs about slavery were ignored. In 1864, when he ran for re-election, he was the candidate of the Union Party and his vice-presidential running mate was an ex-Democrat from the Confederate state of Tennessee. Never for a moment during the war did he consider any peace terms short of unconditional surrender of the Confederacy. He ended his life a sacrifice to the cause of the United States of America.

Of this there can be no doubt—Abraham Lincoln the war president was a true patriot. In words and deeds, posterity's symbol and historical record coincide. But what of Lincoln the party politician prior to his Presidency?

In his creed and in the delineation of his hierarchy of political values, there was continuity throughout his career—always he was the champion of the Federal Union. It is in the realm of deeds that another Lincoln can be discerned—Lincoln the partisan of party.

There have been three good reasons why Lincoln the partisan has not been observed. One has been the blinding light radiating from Lincoln the wartime patriot. The two others stem from what Lincoln did not do. First, Lincoln the political philosopher did not theorize about, and Lincoln the orator did not declaim about, the place of political parties in American democracy. Secondly, Lincoln the political candidate and office-holder was unusually restrained in employing partisan language in his writings and speeches. Because Lincoln the thinker has not confronted the readers of his works with a record of his thoughts about the difficulties of maintaining individuality and independence in a party organization and because Lincoln the practical politician was almost unique among his contemporaries in the scarcity of abusive epithets in his speeches, the importance of party in his career and the degree of partisanship in his positions have been missed by scholars whose very intellectuality predisposes them in favor of a politican who is so different in his use of language—so moderate, so reasonable, and so remarkably literate. . . .

Here are a few facts about Lincoln's party activities that appear in the standard biographies:

Lincoln was a Whig as long as that party had a national party organization. He was Whig candidate for the legislature in 1832, 1834, 1836, 1838, and 1840; he was Whig candidate for speakership of the house in the Illinois legislature in 1838 and 1840; he was Whig candidate for Congress in 1846; he was Whig candidate for the U.S. Senate in 1855. He was Whig presidential elector in 1840 and 1844. He campaigned for every Whig presidential candidate. As a Whig legislator he consistently and regularly voted with the majority in his party on major issues. Despite his antislavery opinions, there is no record that he at any time considered supporting the Liberty Party or the Free Soil Party. Lincoln was not among the leaders who founded the Republican Party in 1854 and 1855. However, after becoming a Republican, he was always a loyal party man. He campaigned for Fremont in 1856, was Republican candidate for the U.S. Senate in 1858, and was nominated for the presidency in 1860 by the national convention of the Republican Party.

That Lincoln was what the Americans call "a regular party man" is an observation that ought to be explicitly stated by writers on Lincoln. Despite its simplicity, such a characterization is highly useful, for it suggests an approach to his career that may throw important light on Lincoln's statesmanship in the crisis of the Union.

Did Lincoln the partisan unwittingly triumph over Lincoln the patriot in the crucial years between 1858 and 1861?

The case against Lincoln's statesmanship during these years centers on his persistence in demanding that Congress prohibit slavery in all U.S. territories, even though the probability that it could be extended into any of them at that time was remote. On August 2, 1858, eighty-five per cent of the voters in Kansas Territory registered their opposition to a pro-slavery constitution. This referendum should have demonstrated beyond cavil that soil and climate would surely attract a majority of antislavery emigrants to the remaining territories, for there was at that time no U.S. territory more likely than Kansas to support slavery.

Lincoln's stand on slavery in the territories in 1858, 1859, and 1860 was doctrinaire. And it was not required by his own moral condemnation of slavery; or at least it was no more required than a demand for abolition of slavery in the Southern states. His own acquiescence in the continuation of slavery where it already existed was as vulnerable to ethical criticism as advocacy of Douglas's doctrine of popular sovereignty by those who believed that antislavery people would populate the remaining territories. Lincoln's moral arguments in behalf of his position in favor of a Congressional ban were sophistical and obscured his strategy of convincing the voters of Illinois and the North that there was a truly significant difference between his own and Douglas's position.

The Republican Party in Illinois in 1858 was threatened by a grave crisis. After Senator Douglas had opposed the pro-slavery Lecompton Constitution in December, 1857, certain Eastern Republicans, notably Horace Greeley of the New York *Tribune* and Congressman Eli Thayer, who had gained national fame for his leadership in the movement to aid antislavery emigration to Kansas, began to express sympathy for the great champion of popular sovereignty and for his idea of letting the people of a territory themselves decide for or against slavery. In Illinois, acceptance of Douglas or his doctrine of popular sovereignty would have been tantamount to surrendering leadership to the opposition and demoralizing the Republican organization built up since 1856. In private correspondence, and even in public speeches, are to be found numerous testimonials of the anxieties of the Republican leaders of Illinois. Lincoln himself voiced his concern vigorously and persistently in 1858 and 1859:

Dec. 28, 1857: "Have they concluded that the republican cause, generally, can be best promoted by sacrificing us here in Illinois?" (letter to Senator Lyman Trumbull of Illinois)

May 27, 1858: ". . . a letter from Mr. Medill of the Chicago *Tribune,* showing the writer to be in great alarm at the prospect North of Republicans going over to Douglas . . ." (letter to Congressman Elihu B. Washburne of Illinois) . . .

Dec. 11, 1858: ". . . the struggle in the whole North will be, as it was in Illinois last summer and fall, whether the Republican party can maintain its identity, or be broken up to form the tail of Douglas's new kite." (letter to Senator Lyman Trumbull) . . .

April 30, 1859: "Had we thrown ourselves into the arms of Douglas, as reelecting him by our votes would have done, the Republican cause would have been annihilated in Illinois, and, as I think, demoralized and prostrated everywhere for years, if not forever." (letter to Salmon P. Chase) . . .

September 16 or 17, 1859: "Last year, as you know, we republicans in Illinois, were advised by numerous, and respectable outsiders to re-elect Douglas to the Senate by our votes. . . . Had we followed the advice, there would now be no Republican party in Illinois, and none, to speak of, anywhere else." (notes for speeches at Columbus and Cincinnati, Ohio)

From a realistic and practical standpoint, a true patriot who was also against the spreading of slavery should have focused his attention above everything else on the probabilities of slavery actually going into the territories. If there was little or no chance of its going into the remaining territories, then surely Douglas's position should have been supported on the grounds that it could command a broader support in all sections of the nation and reduce the risks of precipitating Southern secession.

What then did Lincoln think about the importance of making such an estimate and what was his prediction as to the viability of slavery in the remaining territories?

It should be noted, first of all, that the amount of space that he gave to the practical aspect of the problem in his speeches and writings was small. His speeches of 1858 and 1859 are filled with legal, moral, and historical arguments, but never did he describe and analyze the economic and demographic outlook for the territories of Kansas, Nebraska, Dakota, Washington, Utah, and New Mexico. When he did address himself to the question, he of course asserted that slavery could spread into the territories; he even insinuated, rhetorically, that slavery could spread into the Northern states. Yet, he never declared unequivocally that slavery would surely go into any territory; nor did he ever name one where it would be likely to survive. He merely argued from historical precedents that Negroes could be held in bondage without positive legislation protecting property rights in slavery.

Even in his first inaugural address, where he said that "the only substantial dispute" between North and South was about the extension of slavery, Lincoln refrained from predicting what would happen in the absence of a Congressional ban; he merely said that "one section" believed slavery right and "ought to be extended" while the other believed it wrong and "ought not to be extended." He did *not* say that Southerners believed that it would or could be extended. He did *not* express his own opinion as to whether it would or could be extended.

In 1860, as it had in 1856, the national platform of the Republican Party called for a Congressional prohibition of slavery in all U.S. territories. In the period between his election in November, 1860, and his inauguration in March, 1861, the most important decision Lincoln made was *not* to retreat from the position of the party platform. Despite numerous and intricate arguments of scholars as to Lincoln's intentions and tactics as President-elect, one truth should be crystal clear, namely, that Lincoln never for a moment considered any kind of legislative compromise that might conflict with the Republican Platform of 1860. The evidence is conveniently accessible in Basler's edition of Lincoln's *Works*, volume three:

Nov. 16, 1860: "I am not at liberty to shift my ground—that is out of the question." ("Private and confidential" letter to Nathaniel P. Paschell)

Dec. 10, 1860: "Let there be no compromise on the question of *extending* slavery." ("Private and confidential" letter to Senator Lyman Trumbull of Illinois)

Dec. 11, 1860: "Entertain no proposition for a compromise in regard to the *extension* of slavery." ("Private and confidential" letter to Congressman William Kellogg of Illinois)

Dec. 13, 1860: "Prevent, as far as possible, any of our friends from demoralizing themselves, and our cause, by entertaining propositions for compromise of any sort, on *'slavery extention.'* . . . On that point hold firm, as with a chain of steel." ("Private and confidential" letter to Congressman Elihu B. Washburne of Illinois) . . .

Feb. 1, 1861: "I say now, however, as I have all the while said, that on the territorial question . . . I am inflexible." ("Private and confidential" letter to William H. Seward) . . .

Patriotic statesmanship when Lincoln was elected President of the United States called for endorsement of a legislative compromise. The nation had everything to gain and nothing to lose—except the possible demoralization of the Republican Party. Slavery would not have been extended by the proposals of compromise such as were advocated by President Buchanan and Senator Crittenden of Kentucky—economic realities would have kept slavery out of the remaining territories belonging to the United States. Senator Douglas's proposal to require a two-thirds vote of both houses of Congress to acquire new territory would have prevented extension of slavery into Mexico, Cuba, or other areas to the South. . . .

Whether or not a compromise were accepted by Congress and the Southern states, the advantages of *advocating* a compromise outweighed the disadvantages. If accepted by Congress but rejected by the Southern states, Democrats in the Northern states and in the eight slave states still in the Union throughout the last session of the thirty-sixth Congress (Dec., 1860–March, 1861) would have been impressed by the conciliatory and nonpartisan appeal of Lincoln, and their sympathies for the Confederate states would have been diminished sharply. If accepted by the Southern states, the Union would have been reconstructed peacefully and war postponed.

The United States had everything to gain and nothing to lose by postponement of war. In the succeeding years, the preponderance of the North in population and wealth was bound to become greater. Indeed, Northern superiority might have become so great that the South would never dare to risk war. But if war came at a later date, say 1869 or 1873, the chances for victory would be greater for the North than in 1861, just as they were better in 1861 than they would have been in 1851.

Yet, Lincoln never for a moment considered supporting a legislative compromise! Instead, he held inflexibly to the doctrinaire and sterile position that a law of Congress must be passed to exclude slavery from all U.S. territories. If he had dealt in specifics rather than generalities in his first inaugural, he would have said that the only difference between the two sections about slavery in the territories pertained to the one territory of New Mexico, where, as Webster pointed out in his famous defense of compromise in 1850, legal permission could have done nothing to extend slavery in the absence of economic incentives.

Lincoln in the winter of 1860–1861 did not, like John Adams in 1799, rise above a party position, although the reasons were every bit as compelling as those that moved the President in 1799 to sacrifice the unity of the Federalist Party when he pursued a course desired by only a part of his own party and an overwhelming majority of the opposition.

There is, of course, no evidence that Lincoln thought that he was making a choice between the Union and his party. He was convinced that the position of his party was no threat to Southern interests and institutions; and he repeatedly said so, in language that was easy to comprehend and conciliatory in tone. From

Lincoln's standpoint, all good and reasonable men should see that
the Republican position and continuation of the Southern States
in the Union were compatible; there was just no good reason
why the Southern States should break up the Union rather than
acquiesce in the Republican position, since no practical harm
could possibly flow from it.

There was much truth, of course, in Lincoln's claim that the
South had nothing to fear from his stand on slavery. A bigger
and more important truth, however, is that Lincoln, as the man
in the United States with the greatest authority and responsibility,
ought to have initiated concessions which could not have resulted
in any tangible losses for the North. The fact that Lincoln had
received only 40 per cent of the popular vote was ample justification for his not sticking inflexibly to the party platform.

President-elect Lincoln should have told the American people
that there was no majority party in 1860. He should have told
them that disunion and war ought not to be risked on the basis of
conceivable but remote possibilities. He should have given them
more information and calculations and fewer definitions and pro-
fessions of principle. He should have told them that general
statements about slavery in the territories made in the past, valid
as they may have appeared at one time, meant in 1861 nothing
more nor less than the specific question of slavery in New Mexico
Territory. Confidentially, he should have told Northern Congressmen that his appointing power would be used to assist
economics to keep slavery out of New Mexico; that time was on
the side of the North, that compromise and postponement could
bring no harm, and that they could well afford to make verbal
concessions on a public issue that no longer had a practical importance. What Lincoln ought to have done might have prevented war in 1861. If war should have come anyway, it is doubtful that there would have been a net loss to the nation at large as
a result of an unsuccessful compromise.

3   *Allan Nevins*
      Why Lincoln Said "No"

Lincoln had already made up his mind. Indeed, that central phalanx of the Republican Party which, comprehending not only all radicals but many moderates, believed that the doctrine of the exclusion of slavery from the Territories must be defended as their supreme citadel, was never for a moment moved by the Crittenden Compromise. Lincoln was less likely than anyone else to abandon a principle which he held vital.

On December 10 he had written Lyman Trumbull, who could tell the next Republican caucus: "Let there be no compromise on the question of extending slavery. If there be, all our labor is lost, and ere long, must be done again. . . . The tug has to come, and better now than at any time hereafter." Next day, in response to an inquiry from William Kellogg of the House committee on the crisis, he wrote again: "Entertain no proposition in regard to the extension of slavery. The instant you do they have us under again: all our labor is lost, and sooner or later must be done over." On the thirteenth he sent a similar letter to Elihu B. Washburne: "Prevent, as far as possible, any of our friends from demoralizing themselves and our cause by entertaining propositions for compromise of any sort on 'slavery extension.' There is no possible compromise upon it but which puts us under again, and leaves all our work to do over again. Whether it be a Missouri line or Eli Thayer's popular sovereignty, it is all the same. Let either be done, and immediately filibustering and extending slavery recommences. On that point hold firm, as with a chain of steel."

This was one of the most fateful decisions of Lincoln's career. The reasons why he made it so quickly and emphatically, without consulting others, require a brief analysis.

SOURCE. Reprinted with the permission of Charles Scribner's Sons and the author from *The Emergence of Lincoln,* Volume II, pp. 394–395, 403–404, by Allan Nevins. Copyright 1950 Charles Scribner's Sons.

"They will have us under again; all our work will have to be redone." By this Lincoln meant a good deal more than the naked words assert. It seems safe to say that he had two important ideas in mind. First, he meant that the whole work of his party in winning the election would have to be redone if the victorious candidate immediately surrendered the central tenet of the party. He could yield on peripheral points—not on the expansion of slavery. And Lincoln believed that the expansion of slavery was implicit in the Crittenden Compromise. He told Duff Green that the adoption of the line would still the controversy for the moment, but the quarrel would be renewed by the seizure and attempted annexation of Mexico. Was this unlikely? The South had forced Pierce and Buchanan to take extreme attitudes on Cuba and Mexico. Not only the Knights of the Golden Circle, but a large clandestine organization in California had an eye on Sonora and other territory to the southward. And what if Hawaii were annexed? The Republican Party had been born from a great principle—and now it was asked to sacrifice it under threat and menace. If it did so, how could it face honest Northern voters again?

More fundamentally, Lincoln had in mind his statement that "a crisis must be reached and passed," and the country brought to a completely new resolution respecting slavery. He had said explicitly that the nation as a whole must be persuaded to accept the containment of slavery within existing bounds as a prelude to the blest goal of ultimate extinction. His election on the principle of nonextension constituted the crisis; if the South accepted the election, realizing its import, the crisis *would* be passed; the nation could go on to consider slavery from a more constructive point of view. Its psychology on the great question would rapidly alter. But what if the nation backed away from a decision, and refused to accept the only principle on which a permanent solution, in keeping with nineteenth century progress, could be based? What if it turned back to the old policy of drift? Europe in 1848 had given the world the tragic spectacle of nations coming up to a healthy turningpoint—and refusing to turn. Could the United States afford to do so? Could the one leader who had demanded that the country face the crisis now flinch and bid his party recede? To this question, Lincoln said *No* . . . .

. . . we must bear in mind that the central tenet of the Republican Party, ever since its foundation, had been the exclusion of slavery from all new Territories. We must also bear in mind that to Lincoln this doctrine of the containment of slavery represented much more than an objective, a goal. It represented rather a beginning, a new start. It represented, that is, the point at which one phase in the consideration of the great problems of slavery and race adjustment ended, and another phase began.

Once containment was tacitly accepted by the South, that section must also accept the corollary that slavery was a transitional and not a permanent institution; that the nation must look forward to a time, however distant, when it would be ended; that the country must take some initial step toward gradual abolition, perhaps combined with colonization abroad, and certainly combined with a fair plan of compensation. By arduous labor and heroic sacrifices, beginning in 1846 with the Wilmot Proviso and running through the spasmodic thrust of the Free Soil Party, the organization of the Republicans, their four Congressional campaigns, their two Presidential battles, and a tremendous mobilization of newspapers, orators, and pamphleteers, an Administration had been elected on a platform of containment. It had reached the end of the beginning. And now it was asked to begin all over again!

Such a surrender would have been endurable had it meant only a formal waiving of the interdiction of slavery in the West. After all, a mere handful of slaves could be found in all the Territories of the land. Nobody in his senses supposed that Negroes would ever be carried in any numbers into Nebraska, Dakota, Colorado, and Washington. In all New Mexico, despite favorable legislation, census-takers this year found only twenty-two slaves. On any practical basis, the issue of slavery in the Territories was empty. Nor was it likely, though it was certainly possible, that the Southern expansionists who had signally failed to gain any Cuban, Mexican, or Central American soil during the eight years of Pierce and Buchanan would be able to do so in the near future. Northern opposition would be too dogged and powerful. So far as the actual diffusion of slavery went, the Republicans could have afforded to swallow the Crittenden Compromise—for the possibilities of slavery expansion were near their end.

The psychological and political effects of such an acceptance, however, would in Lincoln's eyes have been disastrous in the extreme. At one blow, all hope of lifting the slavery discussion, so long a futile debate between the positive-evil and positive-good schools and so totally out of key with the aspirations of civilization, to a new, enlightened, and constructive plane, would be ended. For what would be the moral result of accepting the Missouri Compromise extension? Forthwith, the hopes of the slavery extremists would rise anew. They would *toil* to make New Mexico a slave State; they would redouble their filibustering efforts; they would dream, however hopelessly, of Cuba, Lower California, Sonora, and Central America. Instead of changing the climate of opinion, the recent Republican victory would leave it unaltered; instead of seeing a "crisis reached and passed," the country would see the perennial crisis lengthened.

No, the time had come to make a stand. The old American policy of drift, postponement, and politic evasion of fundamental issues would have to be stopped somehow, some day, in some fashion—and the Republican Party was pledged to stop it now. It was committed, in Lincoln's words, to placing the institution of slavery in a position where its ultimate extinction would be generally taken for granted.

To Lincoln, therefore, and all who shared his views, it seemed wise to stand on principle, hoping that it could be peaceably maintained. For great causes, great risks have to be taken. For some high causes, it is well that nations will fight and men gladly die.

4   *Richard N. Current*
Who Was the Aggressor?

"He chose to draw the sword," the *Daily Express* of Petersburg, Virginia, said during the war, "but by a dirty trick succeeded in throwing upon the South the *seeming* blame of firing
the first gun."

This was hardly news to that paper's readers. It passed for
common knowledge, at least in the Confederacy.

When Alexander H. Stephens afterward wrote his book about
"the late war," he had no doubt as to who the real aggressor
had been in 1861. In the book the former Confederate Vice
President conducted an imaginary colloquium:

"Do you mean to say, Mr. Stephens, that the war was in-
augurated by Mr. Lincoln?"

"Most assuredly I do."

"Why, how in the world . . . ?"

"It is a fact that the *first gun* was fired by the Confederates,"
Stephens conceded to his incredulous questioner. Then he
patiently explained: "The *aggressor* in a war is not the *first*
who *uses force* but the first who renders force *necessary*."

On this point Jefferson Davis agreed with his former Vice
President, though the two men agreed about little else. Since
the time of Davis and Stephens, Southern historians have elab-
orated the Confederate view. The most thorough of them,
Charles W. Ramsdell, sums up the charge thus:

"Lincoln, having decided that there was no other way than
war for the salvation of his administration, his party, and the
Union, maneuvered the Confederates into firing the first shot
in order that they, rather than he, should take the blame of
beginning bloodshed."

SOURCE. From *The Lincoln Nobody Knows* by Richard N. Current. Copyright © 1958 by Richard N. Current, pp. 124–129. Used with permission
of McGraw-Hill Book Company and the author.

According to the Ramsdell argument, Davis and the rest of the Confederate leaders desired peace. They were ready to negotiate a settlement. But Lincoln, not so peaceably inclined, refused to deal with them.

During the weeks that followed his inauguration he was beset on two sides. Coercionists demanded that he act to save Fort Sumter. Others counseled him to yield. If he acted, he stood to lose the upper South, if not the border also. If he yielded, he would lose his own party. While he hesitated, his fellow Republicans bickered among themselves, his administration threatened to fall apart, and the country drifted toward ruin. He had to make up his mind soon, before the Sumter garrison was starved out.

At last he hit upon a way out of his dilemma. The thought occurred to him—*must have* occurred to him—that he could induce the Confederates to attack the fort. Then, the flag having been fired upon, he would gain all the benefits of an aroused patriotism. Republicans and Democrats would forget their quarrels of party and faction, the border states would respond with an upsurge of loyalty, and wavering millions throughout the North would rally to the Union cause. The party, the administration, and the Union would be saved.

The stratagem was a shrewd one, worthy of the shrewd man that Lincoln was. He decided to send the expedition and—most cleverly—to give advance notice. A genius with words, he could make them mean different things to different people. This is what he did with the words he addressed to the Governor of South Carolina. To Northerners these words would seem quite innocent. The government was taking groceries to hungry men and would not use force unless it had to. That was all. To Southerners the same words carried a threat, indeed a double threat. First, Sumter was going to be provisioned so it could hold out. Second, if resistance was attempted, arms and men as well as food were going to be supplied!

The notice was timed as carefully as it was phrased. It was delivered on the day that the first ships of the expedition left New York. These could not reach their destination for three days at least, so the Confederates would have plenty of time to take counteraction before the ships arrived. Already the Confederates had news that a sizable expedition was being prepared, and they were left to suppose that the entire force (including the part of it actually being dispatched to Fort Pickens in Florida) was heading for Charleston. With such a large force presumed to be on the way, they had all the more reason for a quick move.

The ruse worked perfectly. True, the expedition neither provisioned nor reinforced Sumter; it gave the garrison no support at all. But that was not the object. The object was to provoke a shot that would rouse the North to fight.

In this Ramsdell thesis there undoubtedly is a certain element of truth, but there is even more that is fallacious. Ramsdell—like Davis, Stephens, and others before him—makes Lincoln appear too much the warmonger, the Confederates too much the unoffending devotees of peace. Ramsdell also pictures Lincoln as too much the controlling force, the Confederates as too much the helpless, passive agents.

After all, the Confederates themselves had something to do with the firing on Fort Sumter.

Even assuming that Lincoln had some kind of "maneuver" in mind, he could not have made it work without the cooperation of the Confederates. And it is fair enough to suppose that the maneuver idea in some form did occur to him, since he received so much advice about decoying the enemy into shooting first, and since he was familiar with the idea as applied to President Polk. But the point is that Lincoln could have had no sure foreknowledge that an expedition, no matter how planned and carried out, would have the desired effect. It might have exactly the opposite effect, and indeed he received counter advice telling him so. . . .

. . . If the Confederates had withheld their fire upon the fort, if they had waited for the arrival of the ships and had merely tried to head them off, and if the fort then had opened fire on the installations in the harbor, the Confederates might have had a rallying cry indeed, a cry that would have won them many friends in the North as well as the border states. . . .

There were still other dangers—for Lincoln. If for any reason his expedition was bungled, and the Confederates waited and withheld their fire, then Lincoln and the Union would suffer a psychological blow. And the expedition was in fact bungled, but of course the Confederates did not withhold their fire.

When they did fire, they did not necessarily become the aggressors because of that. To this extent Stephens was correct. By the same token, however, Lincoln did not necessarily become the aggressor when he sent the expedition.

From the Confederate point of view the United States had made itself the aggressor long before Lincoln acted to reinforce any fort. It was aggression when, on December 26, 1860, Major Anderson moved his troops from Moultrie to the more defensible Sumter. Indeed, it was a continuing act of aggression every day that Union forces remained in Sumter or any other place within the bounds of the Confederacy. And from the Union point of view the Confederacy had committed and was committing aggression by its very claim to existence, to say nothing of its seizures of Federal property, its occupation of Fort Moultrie, and its construction of a semicircle of harbor batteries with Sumter as their target.

There is little reason to suppose, and there was little reason for Lincoln to suppose, that he could escape either war or the charge of warmonger by giving up Sumter and holding Pickens as a substitute symbol of the national authority. The Confederate commissioners in Washington had instructions to obtain the cession of Pickens and other places as well as Sumter. Lincoln's fact-finding emissary to Charleston, Hurlbut, reported back that conflict could not be averted by Sumter's abandonment. "Undoubtedly this will be followed by a demand for Pickens and the Keys of the Gulf," Hurlbut opined. Indeed, Seward himself at the last did not really believe that Pickens, in contrast to Sumter, could be held and reinforced without war. He merely thought a better case for war could be made in consequence of an incident at Pickens. . . .

No matter which way he turned, Lincoln could find no clear and unobstructed path away from the danger of war. As Hurlbut told him, and as various signs indicated, the sacrifice of Sumter would mean no guarantee of continued peace. "Nor do I believe," Hurlbut added, "that any policy which may be adopted by the Government will prevent the possibility of armed collision."

Of course, a surrender to the Confederate demands might have prevented, or at least postponed, the shooting. When the Confederates talked of peace, that is what they meant—a surrender on Lincoln's part. They wanted peace with the recognition of the Confederacy and the transfer to it of all the property the United States claimed within Confederate boundaries. No doubt Lincoln longed for peace. But peace to him was meaningless without the preservation of the Union.

And even if he had been willing to yield all that the seceders for the moment demanded, he had no assurance that the result would be anything more than a postponement of war, a prolongation of the truce. One possibility is this: the rest of the slave states might have remained in the Union, and the seven states of the stunted Confederacy might have had eventually no good choice but to abandon their experiment in rebellion. But there is another possibility: the Union and the Confederacy might have come into conflict over any one of several points, and an incident arising therefrom might have precipitated the secession of the upper South. As a matter of fact, not all the secessionist leaders were satisfied with the extent of the Confederacy as it was at the start. Hotheads in South Carolina—and in Virginia too—hoped for a clash that would bring new members to the Confederacy. A couple of the rabid Virginians, Roger A. Pryor and Edmund Ruffin, went to Charleston before the Sumter attack and did all they could to stir up trouble, with the idea that Virginia would go to South Carolina's aid once trouble came. Lincoln, if he had let the Confederacy have its way in April, 1861, would doubtless have had to contend thereafter with a continuation of this deliberate troublemaking.

Thus Lincoln was far less a plotter of war-bringing maneuvers than some of the Confederates themselves. And he was no more the aggressor in the conflict than any of the Confederates were.

PART TWO

The War Leader

The War Leader

I have heard, in such way as to believe it, of your recently saying that both the Army and the Government needed a Dictator. Of course it was not *for* this, but in spite of it, that I have given you the command. Only those generals who gain successes, can set up dictators. What I now ask of you is military success, and I will risk the dictatorship.

LINCOLN TO GENERAL JOSEPH HOOKER, JANUARY 26, 1863

Mr. Lincoln's perilous task has been to cast a rather shackly raft through the rapids, making fast the unrulier logs as he could snatch opportunity, and the country is to be congratulated that he did not think it his duty to run straight at all hazards, but cautiously to assure himself with his setting-pole where the main current was, and keep steadily to that.

JAMES RUSSELL LOWELL, 1864

Mr. Lincoln, though doubtless one of the greatest men who have ruled the United States, was entirely ignorant of war. Able and wise as he was in all matters of civil government, he failed here most disastrously.

FIELD-MARSHAL VISCOUNT WOLSELEY, 1889

Lincoln had that faculty of intense application and clear insight, so rare that we call it genius; and he applied it as successfully to military affairs as to politics.

GENERAL FRANCIS V. GREENE, 1909

Not until fairly late in Lincoln's presidential tenure did more than a few of his contemporaries begin to suspect that he might be something better than a mediocrity as a war leader. Many Republicans were scarcely less vehement than the Democratic opposition in their criticism of his performance. Military successes in the West and political success in the election of 1864 substantially altered the contemporary view of Lincoln. Then Appomattox and martyrdom made him a figure of heroic proportions—the Great Emancipator and Savior of the Union. The emphasis, however, was upon his civil leadership of the government and the American people. His strictly military role as commander-in-chief was evaluated later and is still a subject of controversy. Lincoln, it has been said, interfered too much in military operations and showed bad judgment in too many of his military appointments. Examples often cited are his decision to withhold McDowell's Corps from the Peninsular Campaign in 1862 and his subsequent choice of Burnside to command the Army of the Potomac. The British military historian, G.F.R. Henderson, attributes Union defeats in the early years of the war to a failure of leadership at the highest level. Probably more influential today, however, is the studied opinion of T. Harry Williams that Lincoln surpassed all of his generals in strategic understanding and proved to be a "great war director." Yet, one question still not entirely settled is whether George B. McClellan might have won the war sooner if Lincoln and the other Northern politicians had given him unqualified support. Richard N. Current summarizes the arguments for and against this most controversial of Union commanders. One of Lincoln's achievements, according to Williams, was the creation of a workable command system in which General Henry W. Halleck at last found his "proper niche" as chief of staff. Previously, Halleck had been a disappointment in the role of general-in-chief, but his biographer, Stephen E. Ambrose, argues that Lincoln made good use of "Old Brains" as a lightning rod for criticism when unpopular dedisions had to be made. Did Lincoln's leadership, then, have a decisive effect on the outcome of the conflict? An affirmative answer by an eminent historian is presented in the final section of this chapter, as David M. Potter measures Jefferson Davis against Lincoln and finds him wanting.

5   G. F. R. Henderson
No Man Is a Born Strategist

In March, 1862, more than 200,000 Federals were prepared to invade Virginia. McClellan, before McDowell was withheld, reckoned on placing 150,000 men at West Point. Frémont, in West Virginia, commanded 30,000, including the force in the Kanawha Valley; and Banks had crossed the Potomac with over 30,000.

Less than 60,000 Confederate soldiers were available to oppose this enormous host, and the numerical disproportion was increased by the vast material resources of the North. . . .

The odds against the South were great; and to those who believed that Providence sides with the big battalions, that numbers, armament, discipline, and tactical efficiency, are all that is required to ensure success, the fall of Richmond must have seemed inevitable.

But within three months of the day that McClellan started for the Peninsula the odds had been much reduced. The Confederates had won no startling victories. Except in the Valley, and there only small detachments were concerned, the fighting had been indecisive. The North had no reason to believe that her soldiers, save only the cavalry, were in any way inferior to their adversaries. And yet, on June 26, where were the "big battalions"? 105,000 men were intrenched within sight of the spires of Richmond; but where were the rest? Where were the 70,000 that should have aided McClellan, have encircled the rebel capital on every side, cut the communications, closed the sources of supply, and have overwhelmed the starving garrison? How came it that Frémont and Banks were no further south than they were in March? that the Shenandoah Valley still poured its produce into Richmond? that McDowell had not yet crossed the Rappahannock? What mysterious power had com-

SOURCE. G. F. R. Henderson, *Stonewall Jackson and the American Civil War* (London: Longmans Green & Co. Ltd., 1906) Vol. I, pp. 404–407.

pelled Lincoln to retain a force larger than the whole Confederate army "to protect the national capital from danger and insult"? It was not hard fighting. The Valley campaign, from Kernstown to Port Republic, had not cost the Federals more than 7,000 men; and, with the exception of Cross Keys, the battles had been well contested. It was not the difficulties of supply or movement. It was not absence of information; for until Jackson vanished from the sight of both friend and foe on June 17, spies and "contrabands" (i.e. fugitive slaves) had done good work. Nor was it want of will on the part of the Northern Government. None were more anxious than Lincoln and Stanton to capture Richmond, to disperse the rebels, and to restore the Union. They had made stupendous efforts to organise a sufficient army. To equip that army as no army had ever been equipped before they had spared neither expense nor labour; and it can hardly be denied that they had created a vast machine, perhaps in part imperfect, but, considering the weakness of the enemy, not ill-adapted for the work before it.

There was but one thing they had overlooked, and that was that their host would require intelligent control. So complete was the mechanism, so simple a matter it appeared to set the machine in motion, and to keep it in the right course, that they believed that their untutored hands, guided by common-sense and sound abilities, were perfectly capable of guiding it, without mishap, to the appointed goal. Men who, aware of their ignorance, would probably have shrunk from assuming charge of a squad of infantry in action, had no hesitation whatever in attempting to direct a mighty army, a task which Napoleon has assured us requires profound study, incessant application, and wide experience.

They were in fact ignorant—and how many statesmen, and even soldiers, are in like case?—that strategy, the art of manœuvring armies, is an art in itself, an art which none may master by the light of nature, but to which, if he is to attain success, a man must serve a long apprenticeship.

The rules of strategy are few and simple. They may be learned in a week. They may be taught by familiar illustrations or a dozen diagrams. But such knowledge will no more teach a man to lead an army like Napoleon than a knowledge of grammar will teach him to write like Gibbon. Lincoln, when the army he had so zealously toiled to organise, reeled back in confusion from Virginia, set himself to learn the art of war. He collected, says his biographer, a great library of military books; and, if it were not pathetic, it would be almost ludicrous, to read of the great President, in the midst of his absorbing labours and his ever-growing anxieties, poring night after night, when his capital was asleep, over the pages of Jomini and Clausewitz. And what was the result? In 1864, when Grant was appointed to the command of the Union armies, he said: "I neither ask nor desire to know anything of your plans. Take the responsibility and act, and call on me for assistance." He had learned at last that no man is a born strategist.

6   T. Harry Williams
A Great Natural Strategist

If a modern poll organization had existed at the beginning of the American Civil War in 1861 and if it had asked which President of the rival governments would make the greater war director, what answer would it have received? Undoubtedly the average informed observer would have predicted that the head of the Southern states would outshine his Northern opponent. Such a judgment seemed justified by the backgrounds of the two men.

Jefferson Davis, President of the Confederate States, was a graduate of the United States Military Academy at West Point, then the only advanced military school in the country. He had served as a combat officer in the Mexican War, and he had been a very effective Secretary of War in President Franklin Pierce's

SOURCE. Reprinted by permission of G. P. Putnam's Sons from *Abraham Lincoln: A New Portrait* edited by Henry B. Kranz. Copyright © 1959 by Henry B. Kranz, pp. 83–90.

Cabinet. Abraham Lincoln had had no military education and no military experience, except for a brief and inconsequential interlude as a militia captain in a small Indian war.

Lincoln always ridiculed his services in the Black Hawk War. In a speech in Congress he mockingly referred to himself as a "military hero," and recalled that he had bent a musket accidentally and made some fierce charges on the wild onions and engaged in many bloody struggles with the mosquitoes. It is possible, however, that his campaign against the Indians gave him a valuable insight into the psychology of the citizen soldier, the kind of men who would compose the armies of the Civil War.

And yet, contrary to all the apparent probabilities, Lincoln turned out to be a great war director and Jefferson Davis a mediocre one. The war records of the two executives demonstrate better than any other example in history the truth of one of Clausewitz's dicta. The great German had said that an acquaintance with military affairs was not the principal qualification for a director of war but that "a remarkable, superior mind and strength of character" were more important. Fortunately for the cause of American nationality, these were qualities that Lincoln possessed in eminent degree.

The American Constitution clearly stated that the President was the commander in chief of the armed forces. Thus Lincoln's authority to direct the Northern war effort was almost unlimited. But if his command position was sharply defined, the command system with which he had to work was loosely and inadequately organized; in fact, in the modern sense it was not a system at all. In the entire military organization there was no agency charged with the function of planning strategy or of integrating strategy with national policy.

The army possessed a body known as the "general staff," but it bore little if any resemblance to a modern staff. The members were the heads of the bureaus in the War Department: the quartermaster general, the chief of ordnance, the adjutant general, and others. This staff held no joint meetings and framed no common plans. Its work was completely technical and administrative, and each bureau head went pretty much his own way with little supervision from above.

Presiding over the staff and the rest of the army organization was the general in chief, the general officer with the senior commission. In 1861 the occupant of this position was Winfield Scott, veteran of the War of 1812 and the Mexican War, who was seventy-five years old and in such bad health that he could hardly walk.

Scott was one of the two officers in the service who before the war had commanded men in numbers large enough to be called an army; the other was John E. Wool, who was two years older than Scott. And the army that Scott had led in the Mexican War numbered only 14,000 men. Small as this force had been, it was the largest aggregation of troops that the younger officers—except a few who had visited Europe—had ever seen. Not one of the junior officers had directed the evolutions of as large a unit as a brigade, and only a handful had administered a regiment.

Most members of the officer corps were able, after the war began, to adjust their thinking to the requirements of the mass armies that came into being. But they had great difficulty in altering their concepts of strategy to meet the realities of modern war. Most American officers were trained in the eighteenth-century tradition of war. War was something that was fought between armies and that did not involve civilian societies; it should be directed by professional soldiers without interference by political officials; and it could be so conducted—by adept maneuver—that victory would result without a showdown battle.

If there had to be a decisive engagement, American soldiers thought it should be fought by the maxims laid down by Henri Jomini, the brilliant Swiss who had served under Napoleon. According to Jomini, or more accurately, according to the American interpretation of him, the largest possible force should be concentrated at one point for one big effort against the enemy.

Most of Lincoln's generals could not understand that many of Jomini's ideas did not apply to their war. In a country as large as the United States and with the North enjoying a distinct numerical superiority, it was possible to mount two or more big offensives simultaneously. And the first Northern generals failed utterly to realize that in a democracy and in a modern war the civilian authorities would insist, and rightly so, on having a voice in the conduct of the conflict.

Almost immediately Lincoln demonstrated that he possessed great natural powers as a strategist. His very first acts were bold and imaginative moves for a man dealing with military questions for the first time. He grasped the importance of naval warfare, and proclaimed a naval blockade of the South. He saw that human and material resources were on his side, and called for the mobilization of over 400,000 men. He understood the advantage that numbers gave the North, and—contrary to Jominian strategy—urged his generals to maintain a constant and relentless pressure on the whole line of the Confederacy until a weak spot was found and a breakthrough could be made. And departing from eighteenth-century concepts, he realized that the principal objective of his armies was to seek contact with the Confederate armies and not to occupy Southern territory.

During the first three years of the war, Lincoln performed many of the functions that in a modern command system would be assigned to the chief of the general staff or to the joint chiefs of staff. He framed policy, devised strategy, and even on occasion directed tactical movements. For this he has been criticized by some writers, who contend that he "interfered" too much with matters outside his proper sphere. But in judging Lincoln's actions, it must be remembered that he operated in the absence of a formal command system. No agency to prepare strategy existed and if Lincoln had not acted no action would have resulted.

Moreover, it was fortunate for the Union cause, in most cases, that he interfered. Many of his alleged interventions were nothing more than attempts to force his generals to fight, to execute the role for which generals and armies supposedly are created. Sometimes Lincoln erred—because he lacked technical military knowledge or because he neglected such mundane problems as supplies and transportation. But the vital point is that even when he was wrong he acted from a sound military basis: to make an offensive strategy more offensive. Conversely, it may be said that Davis's great error was to interfere from a faulty basis: to make a defensive strategy more defensive.

In the beginning months of the war, Lincoln naturally turned to old General Scott for strategic counsel. He soon discovered that Scott lacked the qualities required in a general in chief. All of Scott's experience had been in small wars. Asked by Lincoln to present an over-all plan, Scott came up with a design that called for a naval blockade of the Southern coast and the occupation of the Mississippi River line. The South would be enfolded in a gigantic circle—and with the drawing of the circle Scott would stop. The North could then sit back and wait for the besieged South to yield.

This was the famous "anaconda plan" to squeeze the Confederacy into submission. Although it had obvious merits (the blockade and the Mississippi line became staple items in Northern strategy), it also had basic defects. For one thing, the plan would be a long time in making its possible effects felt. More important, it represented, as Lincoln the civilian saw, the one-weapon or the one-service idea of war. No single strategic procedure was going to win the Civil War.

By November of 1861 Scott had been persuaded to retire. To the post of general in chief Lincoln named George B. McClellan, who was also the field commander of the principal Federal army in the Eastern theater. The young, thirty-five-year-old McClellan demonstrated almost immediately that he did not possess the abilities to plan and direct the movements of a number of armies. At Lincoln's request, he too prepared a strategic design. He proposed that an army of 273,000 men be placed under his command in the Eastern theater. The navy would land this host on the Virginia coast, from whence McClellan would march inland and capture Richmond, the Confederate capital. In a series of similar operations, the army would conquer and occupy the entire Eastern seaboard of the Confederacy.

On almost every count, the plan was defective. It demanded too much of available resources. The government could not have assembled that many men in one theater, or housed and fed them if assembled. Nor did the sea transport exist to take the troops where McClellan wanted to operate. McClellan's scheme, calling for a supreme concentration of effort in one theater, was a complete example of Jominian strategy. Lincoln must have been amazed when he read the document, which he filed safely away without comment.

Outside of this proposal, McClellan indulged in no general strategic planning worthy of the name. When he took the field in the spring of 1862, Lincoln relieved him as general in chief on the grounds that one man could not direct an army engaged in active operations and at the same time plan moves for other armies. The President did not appoint another officer to the position until July.

In the interim Lincoln acted as his own general in chief. There can be little doubt that by this time he had come to have serious misgivings about the professional soldiers. Inclined at first to defer too much to their opinions, he now felt a growing confidence in his own powers to decide military questions, and he was perhaps a little too ready to impose his opinions on the generals.

Nevertheless, in this period Lincoln did not presume to dispense completely with expert advice. Secretary of War Stanton had convened an agency known as the Army Board, consisting of the heads of the bureaus in the War Department. This was only the general staff brought together under a chairman, but the transformation of the bureau chiefs into a collective body was a forward step in command. Lincoln frequently consulted the Board before arriving at an important decision.

Despite his increasing doubts about soldiers, Lincoln seemed to sense that there was something wrong in the existing arrangement. He, a civilian, was doing things that should be done by a military man. Again he decided to fill the post of general in chief. In July, 1862, he named to the position Henry W. Halleck, who had been a departmental commander in the Western theater.

General Halleck seemed to be the ideal man for the job. Before the war he had been known as one of the foremost American students of the art of war, the translator of Jomini into English and an author in his own right. Moreover, he had been a capable departmental administrator. Lincoln intended that Halleck should be a real general in chief, that he should, under the authority of the President, actually plan and direct operations.

At first Halleck acted up to his role—but not for long. His great defect was that he disliked responsibility. He delighted to provide technical knowledge and to advise, but he shrank from making decisions. Gradually he divested himself of his original function and deliberately assumed the part of an adviser and an informed critic.

Halleck's refusal to perform the requirements of his position forced Lincoln to act again as general in chief, but he kept Halleck as titular head of the office. The President had discovered that Halleck could do one valuable service for him—in the area of military communications. Often Lincoln and his generals had had serious misunderstandings because, almost literally, they spoke different languages, Lincoln the words of the lawyer-politician and the generals the jargon of the military. Halleck had lived in both the civil and the military worlds, and he could speak the language of both. Increasingly Lincoln came to entrust the framing of his directives to Halleck.

In those years of lonely responsibility when Lincoln directed the war effort he grew steadily in stature as a strategist. Usually he displayed greater strategic insight than most of his commanders. But he was willing, as he had been earlier, to yield the power to frame and control strategy to any general who could demonstrate that he could do the job—if he could find the general. By 1864 both he and the nation were certain they had found the man—Ulysses S. Grant. And in that year the United States finally achieved a modern command system to fight a modern war.

In the system arrived at in 1864, which was the joint product of Lincoln and Congress, Grant was named general in chief, charged with the function of planning and directing the movements of all Union armies. Grant, because he disliked the political atmosphere of Washington, established his headquarters with the field army in the Eastern theater, but did not technically command that army. In the new arrangement Halleck received a new office, "chief of staff." He was not, however, a chief of staff in today's sense of the term. Primarily he was a channel of communication between Lincoln and Grant and between Grant and the seventeen departmental commanders under Grant. Halleck performed the vital work that in a modern army is done by the secretariat. The perfect office soldier, he had found at last his proper niche.

As a general in chief, Grant justified every belief in his capacities. He possessed in superb degree the ability to think of the war in over-all terms. But his grand plan of operations that ended the war was partly Lincolnian in concept. Grant conformed his strategy to Lincoln's known ideas: Hit the Confederacy from all sides with pulverizing blows and make enemy armies the main objective. The general submitted the broad outlines of his plan to Lincoln, and the President, trusting in Grant, approved the design without seeking to know the details.

The 1864 command system embodied the brilliance of simplicity: a commander in chief to lay down policy and grand strategy, a general in chief to frame specific battle strategy, and a chief of staff to coordinate information. It contained elements that later would be studied by military leaders and students in many nations. Abraham Lincoln, without fully realizing his part, had made a large and permanent contribution to the story of command organization.

7   Richard N. Current
The McClellan Question

The experts have wrangled loudest and longest about the differences which in 1862 developed between Lincoln and McClellan in regard to the management of the fighting on the Virginia front. To make the issues clear, it may help to tell the

SOURCE. From *The Lincoln Nobody Knows* by Richard N. Current pp. 140–151. Copyright © 1958 by Richard N. Current. Used with permission of McGraw-Hill Book Company and the author.

story twice—first from the pro-McClellan, anti-Lincoln view; then from the pro-Lincoln, anti-McClellan side.

Afterward, McClellan wrote in an official report: "In the arrangement and conduct of campaigns the direction should be left to professional soldiers. A statesman may, perhaps, be more competent than a soldier to determine the political objects and direction of a campaign; but those once decided upon, everything should be left to the responsible military head, without interference from civilians."

What had happened to McClellan illustrates the evils of civilian interference at their worst, according to those who dispute Lincoln's greatness as a commander in chief.

Now, McClellan had his faults. Though fond of Napoleonic poses, he lacked the fighting blood of Bonaparte. He was slow, overcautious, duped by his spies' fantastic exaggerations of enemy strength. Yet he had real abilities, particularly in drilling troops and inspiring them with loyalty and trust. To some extent his faults were merely defects of his virtues. He sought to make the most of the Union preponderance in men and resources—to win the war by strategy, not butchery. Gather an army of tremendous numbers, train it to perfection, and equip it with the best. Then, when all is ready, but not a day before, overwhelm the enemy in a single campaign. That was McClellan's idea, and that was the reason for his long delay in taking the field.

His greatest weakness, the one that led to his ultimate undoing, was political, not military. He was a Democrat, a conservative who wished no damage to slave or other property of the civilian South. The Radical Republicans, however, demanded what they called a "vigorous prosecution" of the war, with abolition as a leading aim. They did not want hostilities to end too soon for emancipation, nor did they welcome victory at the hands of a general whose glory would redound to the advantage of the Democratic party. Better years of defeat than a quick success for McClellan, these Radicals believed. So they schemed to frustrate him, working in the Congress through their Committee on the Conduct of the War and in the Cabinet through their two-faced ally Stanton, who pretended all along to be McClellan's friend.

Having put McClellan in supreme command, Lincoln might well have given him a fair, unfettered chance, but the President could not close his ears to the harping of the Radicals. For months he wavered between the self-interested badgering of the politicians and the professional advice of his general in chief. No wonder that, meanwhile, disasters came.

His patience frayed, Lincoln with his General Order Number One commanded McClellan to advance from Washington, setting a day for the movement to begin—and thus, incidentally, betraying his naïveté in military affairs. As if the start of a campaign could be timed by nothing more than a glance at the calendar! McClellan knew, if Lincoln did not, that there were preparations still to be made and that Virginia roads still lay deep in mud.

Lincoln preferred an overland march by way of Manassas (as before, when an ill-trained army went forth to Bull Run and hastily returned) but McClellan proposed to go as far as possible by water, transporting his army down the Potomac River and Chesapeake Bay, landing it on the Peninsula between the York and the James, then moving it against Richmond from the east. His plan had its advantages. It would free him from the dangers of a long communications line through hostile territory. It would enable him, with the cooperation of the Navy, to bring up heavy guns for the bombardment of Richmond. But the plan appeared to have a serious flaw. To nervous civilians, including the President, the plan seemed to uncover Washington, exposing it to capture by the Confederates. McClellan knew better. He knew that the Confederates dared not risk a major blow at the Union capital while their own capital was under siege. And he was going to leave sufficient forces in and around Washington to make it safe against diversionary raids.

Once McClellan had got his Peninsula campaign under way, both the Radical politicians and the Confederate strategists began to play upon Lincoln's fears in the hope of causing the campaign to fail.

The Radicals complained that McClellan had left too few troops behind to garrison the capital. They insinuated that he had done so deliberately and treacherously—to let the rebels take Washington at will. Yielding to the Radical pressure,

Lincoln demoted McClellan from general in chief of all the armies to commander of the Army of the Potomac alone. And he cut McClellan's army, holding back a division and then a whole corps, for the defense of Washington. He simply did not understand McClellan's arrangements for the capital's protection; he counted only the soldiers manning the works in the immediate vicinity, ignoring the force already stationed in the Shenandoah Valley, the one feasible route for a Confederate thrust to the north. The corps he had detached—McDowell's—he placed between Washington and Richmond with the thought that McDowell might cooperate with McClellan by moving toward Richmond while screening Washington. The President appeared to be reverting to his own strategy of an overland approach and doing his best to combine it with McClellan's plan, which he reluctantly had approved.

Then, while McClellan with his weakened army was struggling on the Peninsula, Stonewall Jackson struck with a series of lightning maneuvers at the Union forces in the Valley. Suddenly Lincoln ordered McDowell to turn away from Richmond and go off in pursuit of Stonewall Jackson. McDowell, though himself a Radical in politics, knew the foolishness and futility of such a chase. He protested the order but obeyed it.

As the Washington panic grew, Lincoln wired McClellan about the objective of Jackson: "I think the movement is a general and concerted one, such as would not be if he was acting upon the purpose of a very desperate defense of Richmond. I think the time is near when you must either attack Richmond or give up the job and come to the defense of Washington." Calmly McClellan replied: "The object of the movement is probably to prevent reinforcements being sent me." In a letter to his wife, noting that the President was "terribly scared about Washington," he exclaimed: "Heaven save a country governed by such counsels!"

Lincoln was wrong and McClellan right. Jackson's movement in the Valley was *not* "a general and concerted one" aiming at the capture of Washington. It *was* a diversion intended to keep aid from going to McClellan. Lincoln had fallen—or rather the Radicals had pushed him—into a Confederate trap.

From start to finish he botched the Peninsula campaign for
McClellan. The latter had counted on McDowell's corps for the
specific task of turning the enemy fortifications at Yorktown and
opening the way for the rest of the army to advance up the
Peninsula before the Confederates could mass their forces for
the defense of Richmond. Without McDowell's corps (and without the naval aid he had desired) McClellan felt it necessary to
invest the Yorktown works. Thus he lost a precious month. By
the time he reached the outskirts of Richmond, he had an army
only two-thirds as large as he originally had planned for, an army
scarcely larger than the Confederates now assembled. Yet he
needed at least a three-to-two edge to launch a successful offensive under the circumstances. And he was compelled to deploy
his forces awkwardly on both sides of the Chickahominy River,
since he had to extend his right far to the north so as to make
contact with McDowell, who was supposed to be moving toward
him overland. Even so, McClellan took the worst that Lee could
throw against him. He frustrated Lee's scheme to cut his communications and destroy him in detail. In the course of the
hard-fought Seven Days he saved the bulk of his army and its
supplies and, staging successfully one of the most difficult maneuvers known to warfare, shifted his base in mid-campaign from
the York across the Peninsula to the James. . . .

After the Seven Days McClellan begged for reinforcements
with which to begin an assault upon Richmond from his new
base on the James. But Lincoln could not comprehend the need
for additional troops. Even after visiting McClellan at Harrison's
Landing, he told Stanton that the Army of the Potomac was
"still a large one, and in good condition, although much diminished, consisting when it was sent there of 160,000 men." Later
he made the famous remark that sending men to McClellan's
army was "like shoveling fleas across a barnyard—not half of
them get there." The truth is that Lincoln had not been sending
men to McClellan's army; he had been taking them away. That
army, after its arrival on the Peninsula, never numbered 160,000
or anywhere near so many, though McClellan had planned on a
force of approximately that size, before the President began to
interfere. Lincoln was compounding error with error.

Again the Radical politicians and the Confederate authorities combined to work on the anxieties of the President. The Radicals' favorite, General John Pope, having been given an independent command in northern Virginia, added his voice to the cry that McClellan's army be withdrawn from the Peninsula. And Stonewall Jackson, after having joined in the defense of Richmond, was sent back to the Valley to renew his threats from there. Again Lincoln gave in to his fears, recalling McClellan, calling off his campaign.

Afterward McClellan said that the President, if not satisfied with him, should have left the army where it was, given it adequate reinforcements, and put at its head either Pope or some other general who had the confidence of the administration. For the Federals, as Confederate General Richard Taylor observed in retrospect, "the true line of attack was on the south of the James, where Grant was subsequently forced by the ability of Lee." McClellan was there already, in the summer of 1862. Not for two long and bitter years was a Union army again to be so close to Richmond.

On his return to the Washington area, McClellan became a general without an army, his forces being transferred piecemeal to the command of General Pope. At the second battle of Manassas the boastful Pope was deflated by the foxy generalship of Jackson and Lee. Pope and his Radical friends tried to shift the blame somehow to McClellan, though the latter was without responsibility, and was miles away. In the emergency Lincoln had no choice but to appeal to McClellan and, though receiving no clear-cut authority from the President, McClellan forgot his grievances and heeded only the call of patriotism. He rallied and reorganized Pope's shattered army, pushed energetically through the passes of South Mountain, and met the invading enemy at Antietam. Only the hesitancy of one of his corps commanders, Ambrose E. Burnside, prevented McClellan from coordinating his attack so as to smash beyond repair the smaller army of the bold if not foolhardy Lee. As it was, McClellan in the war's bloodiest day won a strategic success which forced Lee to retreat and headed off a threatened move of European powers to recognize and aid the Confederacy. Not Gettysburg nor Vicksburg but Antietam was the turning point of the Civil War.

"General," said Lincoln to McClellan on a visit to the army camp soon afterward, "you have saved the country. You must remain in command and carry us through to the end."

"That will be impossible," the General replied. "We need time. The influences at Washington will be too strong for you, Mr. President. I will not be allowed the required time for preparation."

That was how McClellan remembered the talk, and that was how the future was to be. Egged on by the Radicals, Lincoln began to complain of McClellan's requests for additional supplies, of his slowness in moving out and making contact with Lee. Lincoln was generous only with advice. Head for Richmond, he suggested. Cut in between Lee and his capital, thus threatening his communication line. The well-meaning President failed to see that if McClellan could threaten Lee's communications, Lee could endanger McClellan's even more. Failed to realize that Lee had an alternative base and was not dependent on Richmond. Failed to understand that marching and countermarching McClellan's cumbrous host was no simple task. Lincoln, it would appear, was an armchair strategist. But Lee, whom McClellan had to face, was not.

Finally, when McClellan was starting out in the direction that Lincoln had indicated, he suddenly was handed a message removing him from all command. Why, nobody really knows, though the Radical clamor had risen to its highest pitch. From a military point of view, the moment was most inopportune. And bad as McClellan's dismissal was, the choice of his successor was even worse. Burnside, the man who had delayed so disastrously at Antietam! In the course of time, by his insane assaults at Fredericksburg (December, 1862), Burnside proved to others what in his heart he had known all along, that he was utterly unfit to lead the Army of the Potomac. After Burnside—Joseph Hooker. And "Fighting Joe" fought little better when his turn came, at Chancellorsville in May of 1863.

If McClellan was a comparatively good general, Lincoln in his dealings with him must have been a correspondingly poor Commander in Chief. And McClellan *was* a good general, according to many a well-informed military man. . . . The man who should have known best, the man who had opposed Grant as well as McClellan, is reported as declaring his opinion in no uncertain terms. When, after Appomattox, he was asked to name the ablest general he had faced in the war, Robert E. Lee did not hesitate. Lee pounded his fist on the desk and exclaimed: "McClellan by all odds!"

And now the other side.

During the Civil War and after, the partisans of Little Mac, including himself, overdid their efforts to make him appear the innocent victim of political discrimination. Lincoln, in his dealings with the general, was guided by considerations of military policy, not by those of party politics.

In his argument with McClellan over the prospective route of the latter's first offensive—directly overland or roundabout by water—Lincoln took the more sensible view. The practical thing to do was to attack and defeat the Confederate army at Manassas, and this was what Lincoln favored. He was not convinced by the case for the Peninsula approach, but he had no general of proved capacity to put in McClellan's place, and he hesitated to impose upon McClellan a plan the latter so obstinately opposed. McClellan's main reason for favoring the Peninsula was this, in his own words: "The roads in that region are passable at all seasons." Supposedly he knew what he was talking about, for was he not an engineering expert? Yet, once he had landed on the Peninsula, he floundered for weeks in mud and bog. Then his tedious cry, his excuse for going so slowly, became the wetness of the accursed terrain.

As for Lincoln's withholding part of the army, this may or may not have been a mistake. Certainly he was right in insisting upon the safety of the capital, for its loss would have been a very serious psychological, political, and diplomatic setback. Perhaps he was wrong in his calculation of the troops available for protecting Washington. If so, McClellan was to blame. He should have taken the President into his confidence, explaining fully and frankly his defensive arrangements. This he did not do. "He

seems to have considered," says Sir Frederick Maurice, 1915–
1918 director of British military operations, "that his ipse dixit
should have been sufficient for Lincoln, whose sole function, as
far as military affairs were concerned, was to comply with his
demands without asking stupid questions." After all, an army
head has some responsibilities in his treatment of the head of
government, as well as the other way around. . . .

McDowell's 35,000 men, if sent on to McClellan, might have
put him in a position to gain a decisive victory, but the question
remains whether he actually would have gone ahead to gain it.
Lincoln had cause to doubt whether McClellan had in him the
aggressiveness to make a determined assault. "Starting from the
premise that McClellan would not attack, it is only a short step to
the next argument," Kenneth P. Williams points out. *"Lincoln
knew that McClellan would not attack."* Why, then, should
Lincoln have wasted additional troops on him?

After the Seven Days the President had all the more reason for
doubting whether McClellan ever would fight a hard-hitting aggressive battle, no matter what reinforcements he might get. The
general insisted that, if given 20,000 fresh troops, he could take
Richmond. He already had about 90,000. By his estimates, however, the enemy before him had 200,000! Even with the reinforcements he demanded, McClellan still, in his own mind, would
be hopelessly outnumbered. Lincoln suspected that, if the Peninsula army were increased to more than 200,000, McClellan even
then would not move. He would double his estimate of enemy
strength, beg for further reinforcements, and wait. No wonder
the President resolved to call off the whole campaign.

If there is any fault to find in Lincoln's handling of military
matters, between McClellan's withdrawal from the Peninsula and
his final dismissal, it is only that Lincoln was too patient in
putting up with McClellan so long and allowing him to act on
plans that Lincoln did not approve. This patience may be inter-
preted as weakness. Or it may be explained by the fact that
there were no clear alternatives, or that there were political
exigencies to be taken into account. The fall elections were
coming up, and many voters might be offended by the removal of
McClellan who, be it remembered, was a Democrat.

Whatever the reasons for his long forebearance (and he for-
bore till after the elections) Lincoln did not dismiss McClellan
because of politics. True, the Radicals were pressuring the President more strongly than ever, but he would have stood unmoved
behind his general if he had thought him the fighting, winning
kind. He did not consider him as capable of treason, despite the
politicians' charges of pro-Southern plotting. No, he got rid of
McClellan for the best of all possible reasons, the one that by
itself was all-sufficient. At last he simply could not escape the
conclusion that McClellan was unfit to command an army in an
offensive undertaking.

The failure of the next two commanders of the Army of the
Potomac, Burnside and Hooker, does nothing to prove that Lincoln should have hung on to McClellan. They are wrong who
say: "McClellan ought not to have been removed unless the
Government were prepared to put in his place some other officer
whom they knew to be at least his equal in capacity." In choosing
his successive commanders Lincoln did the only thing he could.
He chose each one on the basis of previous success in some
independent command, and that was all he had to go on. Mc-
Clellan, Pope, Burnside, Hooker—each had distinguished himself
on some field. And the assumption that McClellan was any
better than the rest of the lot is at least arguable.

The subsequent appraisals of McClellan as a great or even a
good general are worth no more than the judgment of the presumed experts uttering them. In any case, the name of Robert
E. Lee should be stricken from the roster of the eulogists. Though
Lee has been quoted as saying McClellan was the best of the
generals he opposed, the quotation comes not from a contemporary and authentic document but from a second-hand recollection
written down after Lee was dead. There is a good probability
Lee never said it. He did show his opinion of McClellan, however, by his actions in the field against him. It was not a high
opinion. Only against a most unenterprising opponent would
Lee, with his smaller army, have dared to take the risks he did in
front of Richmond and along Antietam Creek.

"Surely the verdict must be: McClellan was not a real general," Kenneth P. Williams concludes. "McClellan was merely an

attractive but vain and unstable man, with considerable military knowledge, who sat a horse well and wanted to be President."

This Lincoln-or-McClellan question is not to be answered by facts alone, though controversialists on each side can prove their opponents wrong, or at least weak, on certain factual points. The answer depends upon inferences as well as facts. It depends upon guesses. We have to guess what McClellan *might have done if* he had been given a full chance, or what Lincoln *must have known* McClellan would do or leave undone.

The Philadelphia newspaperman Alexander K. McClure, once an acquaintance of both Lincoln and McClellan, wrote a generation after Appomatox: "Not until all the lingering personal, political, and military passions of the war shall have perished can the impartial historian tell the true story of Abraham Lincoln's relations to George B. McClellan, nor will the just estimate of McClellan as a military chieftain be recorded until the future historian comes to his task entirely free from the prejudices of the present."

Two more generations now have passed since McClure wrote. He is long dead, as are his contemporaries who took part in the controversies of the Civil War. Those men are dead, but the passions and prejudices of their time are not. McClellan still possesses a rare power to inspire either admiration or contempt, and nowhere in sight as yet is that impartial historian whom McClure looked for.

8   *Stephen E. Ambrose*
A General Used as a Political Buffer

Why, students have often wondered, did Abraham Lincoln keep Henry W. Halleck as his general-in-chief from July, 1862,

SOURCE. Stephen E. Ambrose, "Lincoln and Halleck: A Study in Personal Relations," in *Journal of the Illinois State Historical Society,* LII (1959), pp. 208–216. Reprinted by permission of the publisher and the author.

until March, 1864? Halleck was—diarists, participants and contemporary narrators, as well as later historians, charge—incompetent, inefficient, destitute of originality, afraid to take responsibility and, in general, a hindrance rather than a help to the Union cause. The retention of Halleck has become more mysterious with the growing respect for Lincoln's stature as a military strategist. In despair, Lincoln scholars, generally blind to the reasons for the President's tenacity in holding onto "Old Brains," have almost unanimously decided that Halleck was not worthy of their attention. Through the years, Halleck has become an embarrassment to the Lincoln epic—the single noteworthy exception to Lincoln's ability to select talented advisers.

Thus Colin R. Ballard, in *The Military Genius of Abraham Lincoln,* passed Old Brains off as insignificant. "There is . . . no evidence," he wrote, "that his [Halleck's] advice had any weight either for good or evil in the big questions. . . . [He] dealt chiefly with matters of routine." T. Harry Williams, in *Lincoln and His Generals,* dealt more closely and more objectively with Halleck, but still concluded: "He [Halleck] was supreme commander in name but rarely in fact. . . . His tenure of command . . . did not work out well because he disliked responsibility and did not want to direct." Williams acknowledged that Lincoln learned from the experiment of Halleck as general-in-chief and later used the knowledge, but he did not discuss the reasons for Lincoln's retention of Halleck. Old Brains still remained an embarrassment to the cult of Lincoln scholars.

Actually, the Lincoln-Halleck relationship *adds* significant evidence to the case for Lincoln's genius in selecting and using his subordinates. Halleck was highly valuable to Lincoln as a military adviser—the General-in-chief was one of America's few experts on the art of war. But Halleck's greatest contribution to Lincoln's strength was political. Old Brains allowed Lincoln to use him as a buffer. When Lincoln decided to fire a general or take an unpopular action, he had Halleck sign the order; supporters of the dismissed general (and in the Union Army almost every general had political allies) would blame Halleck for the action.

The "act" convinced spectators, because Lincoln played his part so well; he liked to assume a pose of weakness and simplicity and to give the impression that others were controlling him. When friends inquired about a military move, Lincoln would say, "I wish not to control. That I now leave to Gen. Halleck," or "You must call on Gen. Halleck, who commands. . . ." The general-in-chief usually said nothing. He knew that, as long as Lincoln supported him, his position was unassailable. Besides, he found that he could shape events from behind the scenes, sometimes against Lincoln's wishes—and always in favor of fellow West Pointers when they differed with the political soldiers.

Before he went to Washington in 1862, Halleck saw Lincoln in the same light as did Major General George B. McClellan. The President, Halleck thought, was a typical politician, who, though relatively harmless, was still an incompetent military director.

Never one to place personal pride before country, Lincoln—after appraising Halleck's record in the West—decided to bring him to Washington as general-in-chief. . . . Although Lincoln fretted about Halleck's recent actions, he was impressed by the General's earlier success in the West and by the military knowledge revealed in the General's Book *Elements of Military Art and Science.* Old Brains had decisively proven his administrative ability in St. Louis; yet during the campaign against Corinth, Mississippi, in May, 1862, he had demonstrated an utter lack of any fighting urge. Obviously the General was better fitted for an administrative chair than a saddle. On July 11, 1862, Lincoln made Halleck general-in-chief, commander of all the Union land forces. In less than two weeks Halleck arrived in Washington to assume his duties.

It was the first meeting between the two men, who were to spend so much time together. Lincoln probably was disappointed with the short, pudgy, pop-eyed, middle-aged figure, who looked more like a professor of chemistry (which he had once been) than a dashing soldier. Hiding any feelings he might have had, Lincoln got right to work. He planned to use Halleck, and he began almost as soon as the hand-shaking ceremonies were over, by giving the General a ticklish problem.

The President wanted to remove McClellan and his Army of the Potomac from the unhealthy swamps around the James River, where they had recently been roughly handled by Robert E.

Lee—but if the President, as commander-in-chief, ordered the move, the political repercussions might ruin the administration, for McClellan enjoyed warm, active support from the War Democrats. . . . To Halleck fell the responsibility of making out the order and justifying the action. . . . Lincoln had his cake and was eating it too; McClellan was out of the Peninsula, and Halleck was being damned by the Democrats as McClellan's enemy. Fortunately for the President, Halleck never openly complained or explained the true basis of the command decision. Instead he confined himself to writing to his wife. Lincoln and his advisers had told him to remove McClellan, he said. "In other words they want[ed] me to do what they were afraid to attempt."

Lincoln soon had another opportunity to use Halleck as a political shield. After Pope's defeat at Second Bull Run in August, 1862, Halleck placed McClellan in charge of the demoralized troops streaming into Washington. When McClellan had finished organizing the men in the entrenchments, Halleck asked him who had been nominated for future command. If Lee invaded the North, as he seemed likely to do, the army would have to march out to meet him. But McClellan replied that he had not designated a successor because he was willing to take command in person if the enemy invaded. Halleck informed Little Mac that his authority did not extend beyond the defenses of the capital and that no decision had yet been made as to who would lead the army when it took the field.

Lincoln, however, had decided that McClellan was the only competent general available for command. On the morning of September 2, he and Halleck called upon McClellan at the latter's house. Lincoln diagnosed the situation as bad and, according to Halleck, said to McClellan: "General, you will take command of the forces in the field." McClellan later claimed, probably falsely, that Lincoln had said Washington was lost and asked if he would take over, as a favor to the President. McClellan replied that he would. The whole thing came as a surprise to Halleck.

But Lincoln, after making a decision that angered the very vocal Radicals in his own party, gradually changed his story until the stigma came to rest with Halleck. On the afternoon of September 2, Lincoln told his Cabinet that Halleck had agreed to McClellan's appointment and that the General-in-chief supported the President's views. On September 8 Lincoln told Secretary of the Navy Gideon Welles "that Halleck had turned to McClellan and advised that he should command the troops against the Maryland invasion. 'I could not have done it,' said he [Lincoln], 'for I can never feel confident that he [McClellan] will do anything effectual.' " Two days later the President flatly stated that McClellan's reinstatement was "Halleck's doings." And most political leaders in the capital believed Halleck had decided upon and given the order.

The Lincoln-Halleck relationship reveals more than Lincoln's known abilities as a politician. It also reveals Lincoln's ability to dominate even a man who was supremely confident and accustomed, himself, to dominating others.

9   *David M. Potter*
If the Union and the Confederacy Had Exchanged Presidents

Davis failed in three important ways—in his relations with other Confederate leaders and, with the people, in his fundamental concept of his job as president, and in his specific handling of his politico-military role as commander in chief. In every one of these respects, Lincoln offered a striking contrast and presented superlative qualities of leadership.

Concerning Davis' relations with the Confederate leaders, Clifford Dowdey has remarked that he had only two first-rate

SOURCE. David M. Potter, "Jefferson Davis and the Political Factors in Confederate Defeat," in David Donald, ed., *Why the North Won the Civil War* (Baton Rouge: Louisiana State University Press, 1960) , pp. 102–112. Reprinted by permission of the publisher, the editor and the author.

minds among his advisers—Robert E. Lee and Judah P. Benjamin. Both men had to employ a disproportionate amount of their time and energy in exercising the supreme tact which was necessary in working with Davis. Benjamin was never permitted to bring his originality and resourcefulness into play, and he was forced to forfeit his influence with the public by silently accepting blame for measures which Davis chose not to explain to the people. As for Lee, he was held in peripheral commands or at a desk in Richmond until fourteen of the twenty-seven months during which the South still retained some striking power had passed. Davis never allowed him a post of overall command such as Winfield Scott, George B. McClellan, Henry W. Halleck, and U.S. Grant all enjoyed under Lincoln. When Congress adopted a bill establishing the office of general in chief, intended for Lee, Davis vetoed it.

Compare this record with that of Lincoln, who took both William H. Seward and Salmon Chase into his cabinet, who kept Charles Sumner on his side while at the same time holding border state moderates like Edward Bates, who formed a cabinet with four former Democrats and three former Whigs and blandly remarked that he could balance the elements since he was an old Whig himself. Compare, too, Lincoln's forebearance when Seward was trying to run the administration, Chase was conducting a presidential campaign against Lincoln from his post in the Treasury, and the Blair family was waging its bitter family feuds from the postmaster-general's office. . . .

Just as Davis could not really work with other Confederate leaders, so also he could scarcely even communicate with the people of the Confederacy. He seemed to think in abstractions and to speak in platitudes. . . .

One reason for Davis' failure to communicate was that he could seldom admit he was wrong. He used an excessive share of his energy in contentious and even litigious argument to prove he was right. He seemed to feel that if he were right that was enough; that it was more important to vindicate his own rectitude than to get results. When a matter could not be explained without admitting a mistake, as for instance in the case of the loss of Roanoke Island, it simply did not get explained at all, and the people were alienated by the feeling that the administration dared not trust them with the truth. . . .

The contrast presented by Lincoln shows up clearly in a letter of Lincoln to Grant at the end of the Vicksburg campaign. "When you first reached the vicinity of Vicksburg," said Lincoln, "I never had any faith, except a general hope that you knew better than I, that the Yazoo Pass expedition, and the like, could succeed. When you got below, and took Port Gibson, Grand Gulf, and vicinity, I thought you should go down the river and join General [N.P.] Banks; and when you turned northward east of the Big Black, I feared it was a mistake. I now wish to make the personal acknowledgement that you were right and I was wrong."

This letter has no counterpart in the correspondence of Jefferson Davis . . . .

Davis was a conservative leader, not a revolutionary leader; a man with a strong sense of protocol and convention, but with a weak sense of innovation; a man who was much happier with details than he was with overviews; a man who loved order and logical organization better than he loved results which are achieved by unorthodox methods; above all, a man who thought in terms of principles rather than of possibilities and who cared more about proving he was right than about gaining success.

All these qualities showed up in his handling of his duties as commander in chief. In that role, his other weaknesses were accentuated by his firm conviction that he possessed real military talent and that he should give his attention primarily to the close guidance of the operations of all the Confederate armies. Because of this conviction, he ran the war office himself and all six of his war secretaries were either nonentities or transients—even Benjamin seemingly exercised little initiative while in this post. For the same reason the giant, Lee, was never permitted to hold a general command such as even Halleck held under Lincoln. The same irrestible temptation to run military operations himself also led Davis to descend to points of detail where he lost sight of the larger issues with which he should have concerned himself. . . .

This attention to military detail resulted in something far more serious than the waste of presidential time. It meant that Davis made decisions in Richmond which should have been made in the field and that he hampered his field commanders by limiting their functions too narrowly and by interfering with their command. Not only did he sometimes visit battlefields and change the disposition of regiments while combat raged, but he sometimes sent orders to subordinate generals without consulting, and even without informing, their field commanders.

A striking contrast to Davis' constant intervention appears in the policy of Lincoln, who was always concerned with military policy and often admonished his generals, but who avoided details and refrained from giving orders. Lincoln's whole philosophy was expressed in a letter to Grant in 1864 in which he said, "The particulars of your plans, I neither know nor seek to know." By this statement Lincoln in no sense abdicated his authority as commander in chief. Rather, he clearly defined the true division of function between commander in chief and field commander. His role was to consider overall questions of military policy. The operational particulars were the business of the generals in the field. Lincoln knew this without learning it by experience. Davis never learned it despite his experience at West Point, in the Mexican War, and as secretary of war under Pierce.

If Davis had developed a military policy which would produce victory, his compulsion to run everything himself might not have mattered. But his decision to be his own secretary of war and his own general in chief meant that he was the author of Confederate military policy, and that he incorporated into this policy two fatal principles. One was the principle of departmentalization; the other, allied with it, was the principle of dispersion of force for the defense of territory, rather than concentration of force for the defeat of the enemy.

The principle of departmentalization appealed naturally to a man who thought in formal and static terms rather than in functional and dynamic ones. Like the dedicated bureaucrat that he was, Davis loved a symmetrical table of organization. Consequently, he did not hesitate to carry on the peacetime practice

of assigning the units of the army to completely separate geo-
graphical departments, each one reporting solely to the war office
and each operating independently of all the others. Sometimes
this led to strange results. For instance, Lee, commanding in a
department north of the James, and Beauregard, commanding in
a department south of the James, converged in 1864 to defend
Petersburg, but they continued to communicate with one another
through the War Department in Richmond. But in fact, Lee and
Beauregard did co-operate, despite the mechanical awkwardness
of their situation. What was more serious was that, in general,
the departmental commanders sought reinforcements for their
own departments and looked to the defense of them without
much regard for the needs of their fellows in other departments.
One reason for the loss of Vicksburg was the fact that help had
not come from the Trans-Mississippi Department, and Davis had
rebuked Secretary Randolph for trying to bring help from that
quarter. . . .

When accused of practicing dispersal, Davis denied that this
was his policy, and he might have claimed, in extenuation, that
the state governors exerted great pressure upon him to assign
troops for local defense throughout many parts of the South. But
he was committed to defensive action by temperament, if not by
conviction. He never initiated the daring concentrations which
Lee was willing to risk. He always thought in terms of repelling
the invader rather than of smashing the enemy, and he was slow
to recognize the fearful cost of defending fixed positions, as at
Vicksburg. He never showed the compelling urgency of a man
who knows that time is on the side of the enemy and that victory
must be gained before the enemy's potential strength can be
brought into play.

Once again the contrast with Lincoln is illuminating—and
damaging to Davis. To my mind, it has been conclusively demonstrated that Lincoln had a sounder concept of the overall military
objectives of the Union than any of his generals. He was im-
patient with the endless maneuvering and seeking of positional
objectives which so completely dominated the thought of many of
the generals, and he seldom lost sight of the ultimate goal of
defeating the enemy's forces. T. Harry Williams quotes his mes-

sage to Hooker: "I think Lee's Army, and not *Richmond,* is your true objective point. . . . Fight him when opportunity offers. If he stays where he is, fret him and fret him." Many months later, Lincoln wrote again, this time to General Halleck: "To avoid misunderstanding, let me say that to attempt to fight the enemy slowly back into his intrenchments at Richmond, and then to capture him, is an idea that I have been trying to repudiate for quite a year. . . . I have constantly desired the Army of the Potomac to make Lee's army and not Richmond, its objective point. If our army cannot fall upon the enemy and hurt him where he is, it is plain to me it can gain nothing by attempting to follow him over a succession of entrenched lines into a fortified city."

Many passages might be quoted to underscore the extent of the difference between Lincoln and Davis. But it would be hard to find any quotation which focusses the contrast quite as clearly as Lincoln's statement of what he liked about Ulysses S. Grant. I do not mean his curt: "I can't spare this man; he fights," though that is apposite enough. What I am referring to is his observation: "General Grant is a copious worker and fighter but a very meager writer or telegrapher." If Davis was anything, he was a copious writer and telegrapher—so much so that Pollard said he had ink instead of blood in his veins—and what is more to the point, he seemed to cultivate this quality in his command- ers. But he was a meager worker and fighter in terms of bringing about results, or even of clearly perceiving the results that needed to be brought about.

Fundamentally, Davis always thought in terms of what was right, rather than in terms of how to win. There is no real evidence in all the literature that Davis ever at any one time gave extended consideration to the basic question of what the South would have to do in order to win the war. He said almost nothing on this subject in his messages to Congress, which abounded in passages designed to prove the iniquity of the North and the rectitude of the South. By contrast, Lincoln wanted victory and wanted it so badly that in order to get it he was willing to co-operate with men who had shown they hated him. As he said, "I need success more than I need sympathy and I have not seen so much greater evidence of getting success from my sympathizers than from those who are denounced as the contrary." Lincoln thought of the war as something to be fought, but Davis thought of it as something to be conducted. There was no instinct for the jugular in Davis. That is why one seldom finds him pressing his generals to engage the enemy and never finds him striving for the concentration which might make possible a knockout blow.

In the light of Jefferson Davis' conspicuous lack of an instinct for victory, his lack of a drive and thrust for action and results, his failure to define his own office in terms of what needed to be accomplished, it hardly seems unrealistic to suppose that if the Union and the Confederacy had exchanged presidents with one another, the Confederacy might have won its independence. In this sense, is it not justifiable to doubt that the overwhelming statistical advantages of the North predestined the Confederacy to defeat? Historians have never developed a really satisfactory way of dealing with the relationship between the vast, impersonal, long-range social and economic forces of history and the immediate, close-range, somewhat accidental factors of personality; but here is certainly a case where the factors of personality played an important part in guiding the impact of the impersonal social and economic forces.

PART THREE

The President as Politician

The President as Politician

Lincoln is a figure *sui generis* in the annals of history. No pathos, no idealistic flights of eloquence, no posing, no wrapping himself in the toga of history. He always gives the most significant of his acts the most commonplace form.

KARL MARX, 1862

To become President, Lincoln had had to talk more radically on occasion than he actually felt; to be an effective President, he was compelled to act more conservatively than he wanted.

RICHARD HOFSTADTER, 1948

The secret of Lincoln's success is simple: he was an astute and dexterous operator of the political machine.

DAVID DONALD, 1956

Lincoln never attempted to propose what was more than one step ahead of the great body of political public opinion. But he always led the way.

HARRY V. JAFFA, 1959

Lincoln had a suppleness which Davis lacked, his political experience had taught him how to win a political fight without making personal enemies out of the men he defeated, and he had as well the ability to use the talents of self-assured men who considered themselves his betters.

BRUCE CATTON, 1960

In Abraham Lincoln we have the prototype of the political man in power, with views so moderate as to require the pressure of radicals to stimulate action.

HOWARD ZINN, 1965

In some respects, the radical leaders, rather than Lincoln, proved to be the sentimental idealists and the inept politicians; while Lincoln, rather than the radicals, was not only the hardheaded realist but the most skillful politician of them all.

KENNETH M. STAMPP, 1965

With few exceptions, scholars have tended to place a very high estimate on Lincoln's skill as a politician. Beyond that point of agreement, however, their opinions differ on the measure of his success as a party leader, on the degree to which he was governed by political considerations, and on the moral quality of his major decisions. William B. Hesseltine, a Virginian who spent most of his very productive career at the University of Wisconsin, examines Lincoln's efforts to convert a "conglomeration" into a powerful national party. His most original contribution is the thesis that Lincoln ultimately succeeded in gaining control of the state Republican machines. But the president's political skill was tested primarily in his relations with the Cabinet and Congress. Especially revealing is his successful partnership with Edwin M. Stanton, the able but strange and difficult man who became his second secretary of war. This relationship is analyzed in passages from the estimable biography of Stanton by Benjamin P. Thomas and Harold M. Hyman. Lincoln's relations with the Radical Republicans in Congress have been the subject of an extended scholarly controversy in which T. Harry Williams and David Donald have figured most prominently. The selections in this chapter are taken from the later stages of the debate. Donald, another native Southerner with much Northern experience and a Civil War scholar of the first rank, renews his attack on "the cliché of Lincoln versus the Radicals." He maintains that Williams and other scholars have exaggerated the solidarity of the so-called Radicals, while overlooking the fact that Republicans of all shades were often united and that criticism of Lincoln was almost universal. Donald concludes by offering an alternative explanation of factionalism within the early Republican party. Fawn M. Brodie, biographer of Joseph Smith and Thaddeus Stevens, also disagrees with Williams, but on different grounds. A warm admirer of the Radicals, she defends them by minimizing their differences with Lincoln. In rebuttal, Williams qualifies some of his earlier views but insists that the Radicals were an organized and significant group, revolutionary in temperament and therefore an abnormality in American politics. Their great opponent, he adds, was "the supreme pragmatist in our history."

10 *William B. Hesseltine*
Building a National Party

Lincoln's primary task as a politician was to create a national Republican Party and to mold it into a serviceable tool for the national welfare. The party which nominated him and put him into the White House was an unorganized conglomeration of opposition groups. Some of them had been loco-focos, Barnburners, and then Free Soilers in previous political incarnations. Some were anti-Nebraska Democrats, some were the battered and shattered remnants of the old Whig Party. There were in the undisciplined ranks which marched under the Republican banner, middlewestern farmers who wanted a Homestead law, Pennsylvania iron-mongers hungering for a protective tariff, newly-arrived immigrants and old Know Nothings who wanted nothing to do with each other. The party stood, in common with Breckinridge Democrats, for a Pacific Railroad and for States

SOURCE. William B. Hesseltine, "Abraham Lincoln and the Politicians," in *Civil War History*, VI (1960), pp. 47–52. Reprinted by permission of the publisher.

Rights. It was more certain on what it stood against: It was opposed to Stephen A. Douglas, James Buchanan, the Devil, and the Democrats. . . .

. . . As the election of 1860 drew near, Lincoln advised caution on Republicans. They should not insert into state platforms items which, however popular they might be in a particular locality, would do harm to Republicans elsewhere. He pointed to the anti-foreign sentiment in Massachusetts, the enforcement of the Fugitive Slave Law in New Hampshire and its repeal in Ohio, and squatter sovereignty in Kansas. "In these things there is explosive enough to blow up half a dozen national conventions, if it gets into them." He was not "wedded" to the party platform system, and preferred to have men chosen to office on "their records and antecedents." There was but one item upon which all Republicans were agreed—opposition to the extension of slavery to the territories—and Lincoln succeeded in keeping it to the fore. Yet when he was elected—on a platform which was like a pair of suspenders, long enough for any man and short enough for any boy—Lincoln frequently asserted that the platform bound him to accept its terms and adhere to its provisions.

The mandate of the Republican Party was far from clear, and even had Lincoln attempted to conform to its vague provisions, it would have furnished no practical guide to the political situation which confronted him. There was, in fact, no national Republican Party. There were state parties—and it had been state considerations at Chicago that led the delegates to pass over the party's outstanding man and select Lincoln. Andrew Curtin feared he could not be elected governor of Pennsylvania if Seward were the nominee. Henry S. Lane thought Indiana would vote against him. Richard Yates professed to believe he could not become governor of Illinois on a ticket headed by Seward. Candidate John Andrew of Massachusetts came to Chicago to work against Seward. State, not national consideration nominated Lincoln; and it was state parties that elected him. Twenty-two of the 33 states had an organized Republican Party, and a handful were safelyRepublican with Republican governors and recently successful organizations full of enthusiasm. In eleven crucial states, three in New England and the others stretching westward to the Mississippi, the Republicans had vigorous gubernatorial candidates. In them the national campaign turned on the state elections. Each went Republican, and in each state, except Massachusetts and Illinois, the governor ran ahead of Lincoln. The Republican Party in the states had elected a president for the nation. If Lincoln were to weld a national party, he must first wrest control of its segments from the governors.

Since the governors had elected Lincoln, they had no hesitancy in instructing him on his program. . . . Early in January when newly elected governors, the real or titular heads of the Republican parties, assumed office, they called for war. John Andrew struck a dramatic note in Massachusetts and found echoing response from Austin Blair in Michigan. Richard Yates instructed his constituent who was going to the White House to show firmness and wisdom and to use the military power to defend the constitution. By the time of his inauguration, Lincoln had heard the clear voices of the Republican politicians. The majority of them would brook no compromise with the South and were arming their states for coercion.

The insistence of the governors increased after the new administration began. While Lincoln ignored the governors in distributing patronage, he could not dismiss their demands for action. The Fort Sumter expedition and the subsequent calls for troops, while not dictated by the governors, accorded with their demands. Yet, even as he took an action they demanded, Lincoln seized the initiative from the state political leaders. In the long run, national decisions had to be made by national officers, and Lincoln did not shirk the obligation. . . .

With the initiative in his hands, Lincoln moved to limit the influence of the governors. When, early in May, the governors of western states assembled in Cleveland to urge the administration to greater action and to outline demands for marching boldly to the Gulf of Mexico, Lincoln took them at their word and called for forty regiments of three-year volunteers. These were no state militia called by commanders-in-chief of state troops and loaned temporarily to the government, but federal soldiers subject to the laws of the United States. Without knowing it, or even realizing the political consequences of their acts, the governors raised the troops and commissioned the officers. But they were no longer commanders-in-chief; they were convenient recruiting officers for a growing national army. The generals owed their appointments to the president, and the colonels held their commissions at his pleasure; Lincoln had taken command. . . .

The efforts of the governors to recruit troops brought them increased difficulties both with the government and with their own constituents. Steadily they lost influence, and, with it, much of their political power. John Andrew and other governors, most of them abolitionists, seized upon the hope that they could force the administration to use Negro troops and at the same time advance the abolitionist cause. Andrew and others concocted an elaborate scheme—it really grew into the dimensions of a plot—to raise troops for an army to be commanded by Frémont which would set forth without reference to Lincoln's war to invade the South and arm slaves. To mature the plan, Andrew called the governors to a meeting at Altoona, Pennsylvania, on September 23, 1862. It was no coincidence that Lincoln chose the previous day to issue the preliminary Emancipation Proclamation. The proclamation was a masterstroke of politics, cutting the humanitarian ground from under the state politicians, and leaving them with only the alternative of applauding the president's acts.

Thereafter, both the prestige and the power of the governors ebbed. They had lost the power to direct war policy, lost control of troops as they became recruiting sergeants. Loss of prestige meant loss of political power, and by the elections of 1862 the governors had reason to fear they might be ousted from their offices. Democrats won control of legislatures, and put Horatio Seymour in the governor's chair in Albany. But, even as the state politicians were about to succumb to despair, Lincoln moved to their aid. In the Border States, he had used the army to control elections and to insure the establishment of loyal governments. In 1863 he moved with arbitrary arrests, soldiers at the polls, and soldiers sent home to vote, into the Northern States. In Ohio, Indiana, and Pennsylvania, troops patrolled the polls and insured the election of Republicans. On November 19, 1863, while Lincoln was speaking at Gettysburg, a regiment was supervising a special congressional election in nearby Delaware. By 1864 the troops were ready for political action. In a sufficient number of states to control the electoral college, the army turned the balance between Lincoln and McClellan. And with Lincoln's victory there went the election of the governors. In 1860 the governors, masters of the party in the states, had put Lincoln in the White House. In 1864 the man in the White House, with mastery over a national party, insured the election of the governors.

Building a national party, however, involved more than subordinating the politicians in the states. There were, in addition, the politicians in Congress, and with them Lincoln faced constantly the hated specter of factionalism. In the Senate were Republicans of long experience in both state and national office. William Pitt Fessenden, Charles Sumner, Henry Wilson, Zachariah Chandler, Jacob Collamer, Lyman Trumbull, Benjamin F. Wade, and John P. Hale had long senatorial service behind them, while David Wilmot, John Sherman, and others had been in the House of Representatives. Two senators from Kansas, James H. Lane and Samuel C. Pomeroy, and two from Restored Virginia, John S. Carlile and Waitman Willey, were untried as senators, but fully experienced in the arts of politics. In the House, Galusha Grow, Thaddeus Stevens, John A. Bingham, James M. Ashley, Schuyler Colfax, George W. Julian, Elihu B. Washburn, Owen Lovejoy, and Justin Morrill were well-known and time-tested politicians. They were superior in experience to Abraham Lincoln, who, as Sam Medary saw it, "most unfortunately for the country and his party, had never progressed farther in statesmanship than is learned in the pleasant position of county could practice where wit and wisdom reign more for the amusement of the thing than to *settle* great state questions."

With such political talent in the legislature, Lincoln made no effort to assume leadership in legislation. He had, indeed, no legislative program to promote, and faced none of the problems of the legislative leader who needed to bargain and cajole, to coerce and to compromise to get support for a bill. On the other hand, he had a war to conduct, and needed the support of an integrated national party to bring it to a successful conclusion.

But here he met discordant factions, differing from one another on the purpose of the war, the manner in which it should be fought, and on the results to be obtained. Here he met conciliators who would bargain with the South, moderates who wished to conduct the war with as little social and economic disturbance as possible, and radicals who wished to effect a drastic reorganization of American society at its end.

Fully aware of the contending factions, Lincoln delayed calling Congress into session until four months after his inauguration. Democrats charged then, and the echo has reverberated for a century, that Lincoln precipitated a war in order to save and consolidate the Republican Party. Whatever his purpose, his act gave the party a program and brought conciliators and compromisers among the politicians into line. Moreover, as the people of the North rushed to the mass meetings—and some to the regiments—the politicians could read the signs. "Mr. Lincoln judged wisely" in delaying the assembling of Congress, thought James G. Blaine. "Time was needed for the growth and consolidation of Northern opinion, and that senators and representatives, after the full development of patriotic feeling in the free states, would meet in a frame of mind better suited to the discharge of the weighty duties devolving upon them."

In addition to the desire to use public pressure on the politicians, Lincoln had, in Blaine's opinion, another reason for delaying the assembling of Congress. Kentucky's congressmen had not yet been chosen, and the President desired to "give ample time for canvassing" for the special election on June 20. In the canvass, recounted Blaine, Lincoln "did everything therefore that he could properly do, to aid Kentucky in reaching a conclusion favorable to the Union." In the view of Democrats, who used none of Blaine's mealy-mouthed verbosity to describe the situation, Lincoln went beyond the bounds of propriety in aiding Kentucky. General Jeremiah T. Boyle arrested citizens on the eve of election, and troops at the polls discouraged Democratic voters. The results were heartening to Lincoln. Nine out of Kentucky's ten congressmen were Unionists who could be grateful to Lincoln for their success.

The combination of popular pressure and direct aid, illustrated in the first months of the administration, frequently proved effective devices for dealing with the politicians in Congress. They were not, however, always available to Lincoln. The radical faction, too, used the Union Leagues and the propaganda agencies of the Union League clubs to build up popular pressure for their policies. Moreover, the radicals controlled the Congressional Committee on the Conduct of the War which was at once an investigating body, a fountain-head of radical propaganda, and a pressure group seeking to direct war policy.

With these factional groups Lincoln had to deal. Frequently he found himself forced to yield. Whatever the military merits of George B. McClellan may have been, political necessity demanded his removal from command. Less able and less successful generals—Benjamin Butler and Nathaniel Banks, for example—whose political views were more acceptable to the vociferous radical clique, remained long in command. Whatever the humanitarian or diplomatic advantages of the Emancipation Proclamation may have been, its issuance and its timing constituted a yielding to the politicians in state and national capitols.

Yet, Abraham Lincoln was not the pliant tool of the radical faction. He yielded to political necessity, but he was apt in evading the demands of the politicians and ingenious in diverting them. He handled the Chase-Seward imbroglio in his cabinet with dexterity, took advantage of the premature announcement of Chase's hopes in the Pomeroy Circular, and released Chase from his cabinet after the political danger was passed. He used state legislators and Montgomery Blair's corps of postmasters to launch a "grass roots" demand for his own renomination. He bargained for Frémont's removal during the campaign of 1864. He was a master politician, using the patronage, the army, the ability to appeal to the people over the heads of the politicians, and a shrewd capacity to bargain to build a national party and to keep rival politicians from open and overt revolt.

His most serious problem, and his nearest defeat came on the issues of reconstruction. His plans were many, and each was political in orientation and looked to the eventual establishment of proper practical relations between the seceded states and the national government. Beginning with the Border States, where Lincoln fostered Unionist parties and encouraged the replacement of disloyal governors, his program developed through the establishment of military governors to the eventual announcement of a full-blown Proclamation of Amnesty and Reconstruction. From the beginning, Democratic critics pointed out that Lincoln's plans were political and designed to create a personal party, supported by the army. In the opinion of the Columbus *Crisis,* all of Lincoln's acts revealed "settled designs upon the rights of the states and the liberties of the people." Certainly, Lincoln had no program for restoring the old rights of the states or of restoring the *old* federal union. He was waging a war against the states, and was building a national party. He watched patiently while Andrew Johnson labored in Tennessee to create a political party before he tried to restore the machinery of government. He gave free reign to Butler and Banks in New Orleans as they sought for a loyal nucleus about which to gather a party.

When Lincoln issued his proclamation of Amnesty and Reconstruction in December, 1863, the Democrats were quick to see its political significance. "As a party manifesto," pronounced the New York *World,* "it is a creditable specimen of political dexterity. It trims with marvelous dexterity between the two factions of the Republican party." It was, in fact, "Mr. Lincoln's trump card for the presidential nomination." Other Democrats were more apt in spelling out the details, and soon they were counting the number of voters who would be needed to carry the states of the South. The movement, said the *World,* was not "discreditable to Mr. Lincoln's shrewdness as a politician. . . . There could not be a shrewder device for enabling President Lincoln to re-elect himself." The one-tenth who would take the "abolition oath" would cast the electoral votes of the Southern states. When a military expedition went off to Florida, the *World* saw the movement was not military, but political: "The object was to make it a rotten-borough state under the amnesty proclamation, so that it could throw its electoral vote for Mr. Lincoln."

The radical politicians of Congress hardly needed instruction from the Democrats on the political meaning of the Amnesty Proclamation. Long had they favored a program of conquest which would insure far reaching social and economic changes in the South. They approved Ben Butler's harsh regime in New

Orleans as they saw him destroying the Southern economic system and organizing a new electorate. They approved the social experiments in the Sea Islands of Carolina where the army, treasury officials, and agents of humanitarian societies quarrelled with each other as they sought to combine a reorganization of society with the production of cotton. They saw, as quickly as the Democrats, that Lincoln's plans embodied the personal control over the Southern states. When congressmen from a reconstructed government in Arkansas arrived in Washington, radical Henry Winter Davis denounced Lincoln's proclamation as "a grave usurpation upon the legislative authority of the people." Soon Davis had ready a bill for a more complicated process of reconstruction than Lincoln contemplated, and the members of Congress turned to denouncing Lincoln and his schemes. In the Senate, where reconstruction policies were a constant subject of debate, the Davis bill received little specific attention. The final passage of the Wade-Davis Bill was done with so little enthusiasm that Lincoln had no hesitancy in giving it a pocket veto and accompanying it with a fresh declaration of his own policy.

Radicals Wade and Davis issued a "manifesto" denouncing presidential usurpation, and thereafter, until the end of his life, the radical politicians harassed Lincoln on the issues of reconstruction. The election of 1864 brought success to the Republicans without recourse to the electoral votes of the "rotten-borough" states, and in the congressional session of 1864–65, Charles Sumner filibustered against the recognition of a reconstructed government in Louisiana. On the issue, Lincoln was forced to retreat, and he spent his last weeks devising new schemes of reconstruction. The new schemes never matured, and Andrew Johnson inherited the problem and faced the determined and well-organized politicians of congress.

The end was inconclusive. Lincoln had, indeed, built a national party. He had used the patronage, the prestige of his position, the army, and skillful popular appeals to subordinate the state parties and mold them into national unity. He had had less success in combatting factionalism at the national level, had not succeeded in winning undisputed control over the party he had created. He might, indeed, have recalled his early definition of politicians as "a set of men who have interests aside from the interests of the people, and who, to say the most of them, are taken as a mass, at least one long step removed from honest men." And, had he remembered this, he might also have recalled, as he surveyed his own substantial accomplishments, that he had also added—"being a politician myself. . ."

11 Benjamin P. Thomas and Harold M. Hyman
Working with Stanton

Something in Lincoln's calm, warm, mystical character drew Stanton out of the self-centered shell which he had built around his life. Lincoln's shrewd judgments on men and exploitations of power impressed Stanton. His devout concern for human beings echoed far back into Stanton's youth. Lincoln's conviction that the American experiment in democracy was worthy of survival and sacrifice brought Stanton to action to sustain the conviction. Stanton's early contempt for Lincoln gave way to respect, and then to love. . . .

Lincoln spent more time with Stanton than with any other cabinet officer. This close association aroused the jealousy of Welles, Blair, and Chase, and perhaps this subdued but intense competition for first place in the President's heart accounts for some of the acrimony that existed among the cabinet officers. Almost every man who served Lincoln loved him; that Stanton received the warmest response was his treasured and private reward for his efforts.

To be sure, Lincoln's preference for Stanton's company may have been due in part to his desire to oversee his volcanic "Mars," and also to the monopoly Stanton kept over the military telegraph.

SOURCE. Condensed from *Stanton: The Life and Times of Lincoln's Secretary of War,* by Benjamin P. Thomas and Harold M. Hyman, pp. 382–391. Copyright © 1962 by Alfred A. Knopf, Inc. Reprinted by permission of the publisher.

Lincoln was at the War Department as often as he could be, and at critical times he and Stanton rarely left the place. The President was a familiar sight to the guards Stanton kept posted around the White House—striding in his long, awkward gait to the rickety turnstile that separated the two buildings, hurrying back to a reception or dinner he had deserted in order to slip over to see Stanton and read the dispatches.

Though the relationship between them was not as amiable as that between Lincoln and Seward, it was more intimate. Stanton and Lincoln virtually conducted the war together, whereas Seward had a free hand in managing the State Department except when a diplomatic crisis threatened. Lincoln, Seward told diplomat John Bigelow in 1867, "was the War Minister, and a very good one."

Lincoln was calm, unruffled, careless with secrets, forgiving, inclined to tell a joke to place matters in perspective; Stanton was seemingly merciless, secretive, implacable with error, furious at reverses. Congressman Dawes observed of them: "The one sorrowed over the calamities of war; the other sorrowed that more was not achieved by it." Heart and head of the war, was the way telegrapher Bates thought of the two men, and he insisted that they never really were at odds. "Stanton required a man like Lincoln to manage him," Grant said years later. Lincoln dominated Stanton by "that gentle firmness." Sometimes too forebearing, Lincoln was frequently saved from error by Stanton's strict sense of duty. There were times when Lincoln overrode Stanton, as in appointing officials to the War Department and officers to the Army. Other times the President found himself imposed upon. Yet the two men worked well together on the whole, and counterbalanced each other's faults. . . .

Whenever affairs came to an impasse between them, it was Lincoln's will that controlled, and the phrase "I yield to whatever the President may think best for the service" is in one form or another widely distributed through more than three years' accumulation of memoranda and notes between the two men. When Stanton saw a specific order in Lincoln's handwriting, he knew that his own objections to an appointment, a contract, or a policy had been overruled, and though he fretted, he did not fail to comply with the President's decision. Until that moment, however, he felt free to try to sway Lincoln as much as he could, and to insulate him if possible from too persuasive petitioners. . . .

Lincoln's sense of humor and his utter lack of toploftiness facilitated his relations with the plain-spoken Secretary. Once when Lincoln sent a petitioner to Stanton with a written order complying with his request, the man came back to report that Stanton had not only refused to execute the order but had called Lincoln a damn fool. Lincoln, in mock astonishment, asked: "Did Stanton call me a damn fool?" Being reassured on that point, the President remarked drolly: "Well, I guess I had better step over and see Stanton about this. Stanton is usually right."

He and Stanton each realized that what one said of the other would be rapidly circulated. The President knew that Stanton was "terribly in earnest," and Stanton knew that until Lincoln decided on a matter, he could protest as outspokenly as he wished. Lincoln was willing to circumvent the stubborn Stanton in matters which he felt were important enough, knowing that the War Secretary would finally accept the decision. Robert Lincoln and Ward Hill Lamon, Lincoln's old friend, remembered the unwritten understanding between the two men—each could veto the other's acts, but Lincoln was to rule when he felt it necessary. Important and importunate demands that Lincoln could not refuse, he turned over to Stanton, who accepted the onus of saying no.

On the other hand, when Stanton received meritorious requests that he ached to grant, but feared that an unbearable precedent might thus be set, he referred them to the White House. A Baltimore delegation asked him for the release of a clergyman imprisoned for disloyalty, on the grounds that the man's pregnant wife would die unless her husband was released. Stanton sent the Marylanders to see Lincoln, knowing that the President would be touched, as he had been, and order the release. In such instances Stanton deliberately kept his harsh reputation, but pointed the way to mercy.

Informed Washingtonians knew how to bypass Stanton. When Savannah was taken and starvation faced the inhabitants, New

Yorkers assembled relief supplies and Treasury officer Chittenden approached Stanton for a pass to forward the materials to Georgia. No, the Secretary replied; the war was not yet won: "To exhaust the supplies of the enemy is one of the objects we are trying to accomplish; it is one of the most effectual means of making war. . . . Why do you ask me to do what you would not do yourself in my place? I will not do it. If the people of New York want to feed anybody, let them send their gifts to the starving prisoners from the Andersonville stockade."

Chittenden "could not answer the Secretary," but previous encounters had taught him what to do. He went to Lincoln.

"Stanton is right," the President decided, "but the Georgians must not be left to starve, if some of them do starve our prisoners." And so the supplies went off; although, in order not to "offend Stanton unless I can make something by the transaction," Lincoln had Chittenden accompany them to report on the attitudes of the newly conquered Southerners toward the victorious North.

The President's sensitivity to subtle stimuli that the War Department ignored seemed to drive Stanton to distraction. Lincoln's propensity to delay important decisions as long as possible rubbed harshly against Stanton's taut impatience. Lincoln often clothed in seeming ambivalence his hopes that grave public matters might, by the passage of time, resolve themselves without official interference. He "talks as many ways as he has fears, impulses, & fancies," newsman Barnett reported. These habits of the President sent Stanton into pungent rages. But the important element for their relationship, and for the nation, was that Stanton cooled as quickly as he had ignited. Lincoln had his way, and Stanton adapted his own desires to the wishes of the great man he served.

12   *David Donald*
Lincoln vs. the Radicals: A Cliche

In the political history of the Civil War one of the most widely held . . . stereotypes is the cliché of Lincoln versus the Radicals. The most serious opponents of President Lincoln, so the story goes, were not the Democrats or even the Confederates but the "Jacobin" members of his own party. "Aggressive, vindictive, and narrowly sectional," these Radicals "welcomed the outbreak of civil war as the longed-for opportunity to destroy slavery and to drive the 'slave traders' from the national temple." Once the war came, they stood "for instant emancipation, the confiscation of 'rebel' property, the use of colored soldiers, civil and, when it should become expedient, political equality for the Negro." Behind their antislavery zeal lay their desire to "fasten Republican political and economic control upon the South"; they expected to enact a high protective tariff that would foster monopoly, to pass a homestead law that would invite speculators to loot the public domain, and to subsidize a transcontinental railroad that would offer infinite opportunities for jobbery. Before the war Southern planters had been the chief obstacle in the path of their plans. Now that the Southerners had withdrawn from the Union, the Radicals vowed never to readmit them until their political and economic power was broken. As Wendell Phillips pledged, "The whole social system of the Gulf states is to be taken to pieces; every bit of it."

The Conservative President of the United States, so the cliché runs, opposed these schemes. Lincoln was determined to keep the Civil War from becoming a social revolution. As genuinely antislavery as the Radicals, he advocated the "gradual extinction

SOURCE. David Donald, "Devils Facing Zionwards," in Grady McWhiney, ed., *Grant, Lee, Lincoln and the Radicals* (Evanston, Illinois: Northwestern University Press, 1964) , pp. 72–88. Reprinted by permission of the publisher, the editor and the author.

of slavery, compensated emancipation, and colonization of the Negroes in another land." He looked for a prompt restoration of the seceded states to the Union.

Master politicians, the Radicals skillfully undermined the President's program. They hounded his military and civilian advisers who did not share their Radical views. Fearing that General George B. McClellan would end the war without ending slavery, they worked assiduously for his removal from command; similarly in the west they secured the dismissal of Don Carlos Buell. Of the members of the cabinet they unsparingly denounced Seward, Bates, and Welles, and they forced the resignation of Montgomery Blair. Toward the President himself their hostility was unceasing. The bolder among them sneered at him as a baboon; others characterized his administration as being marked by "epaulettes and apathy, imbecility and treachery, idiocy and ignorance, sacrifice on the part of the people, supineness on the part of the Government." They vigorously opposed the renomination of Lincoln in 1864. "I hope," wrote Congressman James A. Garfield in disgust, "we may not be compelled to push him four years more." Even after the Chase boom failed, the Frémont movement collapsed, and the Republican convention renominated Lincoln, these Jacobins still hoped to replace him with a genuinely Radical candidate.

As to the outcome of this titanic struggle, which clearly prolonged the war by dividing the Northern people and by strengthening Southern resistance, historians differ. Some note that Lincoln in effect nullified the Radical program of confiscation, issued as weak and ineffectual a proclamation of emancipation as possible, sapped the powers of the Radical war governors, and broadened the conservative base of his support by converting the Republican into the Union party; he was thus, by 1865, in an admirable position to push for the adoption of his reconstruction program. Other writers argue that the Radicals were clearly winning. They secured the ousting of McClellan, the abolition of slavery, and the defeat of schemes to readmit the Southern states. Lincoln, declares Professor T. Harry Williams, "surrendered to the conquering Jacobins in every controversy before they could publicly inflict upon him a damaging reverse. Like the fair

Lucretia threatened with ravishment, he averted his fate by instant compliance."

So goes the cliché. There is a good deal to be said for it.
Whatever its deficiencies, the picture of Lincoln battling the
Radicals has been a useful corrective to the bland historiography
of the post-Civil War Republican era, when Nicolay and Hay
could write of Lincoln's renomination in 1864 as a certainty, since
"the general drift of opinion was altogether in favor of intrusting
to Mr. Lincoln the continuation of the work which he had thus
far so well conducted." . . .

Further, one must note in fairness that this cliché is not the
invention of . . . later historians. The terms "Radical" and
"Conservative" were widely used during the Civil War years to
characterize Republican factions. For example, Senator Orville
H. Browning wrote in his diary of "These ultra, radical, un-
reasoning men who raised the insane cry of on to Richmond in
July 1861, and have kept up a war on our generals ever since—
who forced thro the confiscation bills, and extorted from the
President the [emancipation] proclamation and lost him the confidence of the country"; they were, Browning held, Lincoln's
"bitterest enemies, . . . doing all in their power to break him
down."

It should be added that, whatever the truth of the cliché of
President versus Radicals, it does cast an important light upon
Lincoln's own mind. Though the President was careful to avoid
an open break with his critics and squelched a newspaper story
which had him speaking of the "Jacobinism of Congress," it is
nevertheless clear that he often felt himself at loggerheads with
Radical opponents. In ungarded moments he spoke of "the
petulant and vicious fretfulness of many Radicals," and he told
Attorney-General Bates that some of their plots "were almost
fiendish." Doubtless the President got a great deal of satisfaction
in thus personalizing the opposition to his administration.

For all its usefulness and general acceptance, the picture of
Lincoln battling the Radicals may be less a photograph than a
caricature. Historians are curiously imprecise in explaining just
who these Radical opponents of Lincoln were. Virtually all
agree that the group should include Charles Sumner, that classi-

cal ornament of the Republican party; dour, embittered Thaddeus Stevens; the ambitious, calculating Salmon P. Chase; and blunt Benjamin F. Wade. In addition, the names of Henry Winter Davis, Benjamin F. Butler, Wendell Phillips, Zachariah Chandler, and George W. Julian are usually mentioned. But beyond this nucleus, membership in the Radical club is vague. Does a figure like Lyman Trumbull belong? He participated in virtually all of the so-called anti-Lincoln maneuvers of the Radicals during the first three years of the war—only to emerge in 1865 as the chief senatorial defender of Lincoln's reconstruction program. What does one do about John A. Andrew and William Pitt Fessenden, both presumably harsh Radical opponents of Lincoln's who became important spokesmen for sectional reconciliation and for Lincolnian generosity after Appomattox? Even more difficult to classify is Andrew Johnson, who participated eagerly in the anti-Lincoln Committee on the Conduct of the War, only to become the pro-Lincoln military governor of Tennessee and Lincoln's hand-picked vice-presidential candidate in 1864.

To identify the Conservative Republican opponents of these Radicals is even more puzzling. Since virtually all writers speak of the Radicals as a coterie or a cabal, the clear implication is that the Conservatives were in a majority. Yet when one begins to search he can find only William H. Seward, who was largely out of politics during the war years, and political ciphers like Gideon Welles and James Dixon. The principal Conservative Republican in Congress bore the revealing name of Doolittle.

Since there is difficulty in ascertaining just who the Radicals were, it is obviously not easy to learn what views they held in common. . . .

To be sure, all Radicals were antislavery men—as, indeed, were most Northerners of all parties—but they differed as to how the South's peculiar institution should be eradicated. . . . Once the war broke out, Greeley and Sumner urged President Lincoln to free all the slaves in order to crush the rebellion. . . . But the equally Radical Chase, on the other hand, favored a proclamation which would attack slavery "where it has done most mischief and where its extinction will do most good in weakening rebellion and incidentally otherwise in the extreme South," rather than a general emancipation. Nor did Radicals agree on the future of the Negro at the end of the war. Sumner moved slowly and reluctantly toward enfranchising all the former slaves only when he found there was no chance of imposing a general educational test upon all Southern voters; Chase boldly favored Negro suffrage in principle. As to reconstruction policies as a whole, there were material differences between Sumner's "state suicide" theory and Stevens' "conquered province" idea—and neither view was entirely acceptable to other leading Radicals.

Even more shaky is the customary generalization that the Radicals shared a plan to promote the manufacturing and banking interests of the Northeast. To be sure, most of them supported the tariff increases of the Civil War years, though Sumner had intellectual reservations about protection and Greeley claimed that he wanted high tariffs as a step toward ultimate free trade. Many Radicals, especially those who had once been Whigs, strongly favored government grants for internal improvements and of course supported the proposed transcontinental railroad, but Radical Senator Grimes called it "monstrous" to create a railroad monopoly, to which the United States government would give "such beneficent advantages, prerogatives, and privileges."
. . .

Financial questions exposed sharp differences among the Radicals. Secretary Chase's national banking bill, which is correctly viewed as a measure favoring the creditor interests of the Northeast, received the votes of most Radicals, but both Thaddeus Stevens and Grimes thought it a mistake. Some of the Radicals abhorred inflation and urged a prompt return to specie payments, but Radicals Wade, Butler, and Stevens all championed greenback inflation. . . .

This is not to argue that the Radicals shared no ideas. On most issues they saw eye to eye—but not merely with other Radicals, but with Republicans of all persuasions. Too often it is forgotten that all Republicans disliked slavery and that virtually all realized from the beginning that war would put an end to it. Sumner's Radical view that the war offered the perfect opportunity for completing the antislavery crusade was shared by his Conservative rival, Charles Francis Adams, who declared flatly, "The slave question must be settled this time once for all." Both opinions were mild in comparison with the plan of the extremely Conservative Orville H. Browning, who wanted to "subjugate the South, establish a black republic in lieu of the exterminated whites, and extend a protectorate over them while they raised our cotton."

Too many historians have failed to look at the voting patterns of the Civil War Congresses. These show, not Republican factionalism but an extraordinary degree of Republican unanimity upon all measures designed to win the war, and especially upon all measures attacking slavery. The First Confiscation Act of 1861, often taken as the opening gun in the Radicals' war upon the South, passed the Senate without a division; in the House it received the support of 59 Republicans and was opposed by only 9. The more stringent Second Confiscation Act of 1862, highly objectionable to President Lincoln, was backed by 82 Republicans in the House and was opposed by only 5, 4 of whom came from the Border States. . . . No Republican in either House or Senate opposed the Thirteenth Amendment, ending slavery throughout the land, when it came to a vote in 1864; when it was once more brought before Congress in January, 1865, again every voting Republican in the House supported it.

Even on the more controversial issues of reconstruction there was astonishing Republican unity. Only 6 Republicans in the House of Representatives voted against the Wade-Davis bill, designed to take the reconstruction process out of the hands of President Lincoln; 5 of these came from Border States. In the Senate 24 Republicans, including such alleged Conservatives as Doolittle and Henderson, supported the measure; none voted against it. On the crucial proposal to admit Lincoln's reconstructed government of Arkansas, only 5 Republicans in the Senate backed the President; 20 voted to exclude the Arkansas senators.

Similarly, the military views of the Radicals were shared by nearly all Republicans. Radical hostility to General McClellan is well known and elaborately documented, but equally authentic are Seward's protests against the general's "imbecility," Bates's complaints of his "criminal tardiness," "fatuous apathy," and "grotesque egotism," and Lincoln's own animadversions upon his slowness and his unwillingness to fight.

Nor were the Radicals alone in deploring the weakness and incompetence of the Lincoln administration. It is instructive to select a few passages dealing with this issue from one of the most famous Civil War diaries. The Lincoln administration, complained the author, "has no system—no unity—no account-ability—no subordination." The government was "lamentably deficient in the lack of unity and co-action." . . . Indeed, the President, "an excellent man, and, in the main wise," simply lacked "*will* and *purpose*" and had "not *the power to command.*" . . . The author of these remarks . . . was the extremely Con-servative Edward Bates, Lincoln's own attorney-general. . . .

The cliché of Lincoln versus the Radicals, then, rests upon imprecise definition of terms and upon insufficient analysis of the evidence. It fails to define who the Radicals were; it fails to account for their very considerable differences of opinion; and it fails to recognize that most of their shared beliefs were also common to all Republicans.

Inevitably one is tempted to ask why such a shaky thesis should find support among distinguished historians noted for their careful scholarship. Their error, if it be one, clearly does not stem from shoddy research. Instead, one may suggest, the fault derives from what Oliver Wendell Holmes used to call an un-stated major premise. Virtually all the writers who have devel-oped this theme have agreed that Abraham Lincoln's program of conducting the war and winning the peace was sound, sensible, and statesmanlike. With this assumption, they have found it difficult to accept the fact that criticism of the Lincoln administra-tion stemmed from widespread and realistic discontent with the policies of the government; instead, they have attributed anti-Lincoln sentiment to the activities of a little group of willful Radicals.

Whatever the truth of this interpretation, it shares the usual failing of historical hindsight; it does not take into account the feelings of the actual participants in the Civil War crisis. Instead of viewing the period retrospectively, from a vantage point where

Lincoln's reputation is beyond historical assault, it might be helpful to reconstruct the situation as a public-spirited, informed Northerner would have been obliged to see it during the war years. Such a citizen when he read his daily paper would see little evidence of Lincolnian wisdom. Instead, his headlines told him that his government was corruptly and inefficiently managed and that it was an inept and disorganized bureaucracy.

At the head of that ineffective government he would see a well-meaning but incompetent President, who appeared to lack even political astuteness. Few contemporaries could discern much evidence of Lincoln's vaunted political sagacity. . . .

Nor was there much to be said in favor of Lincoln's military policy, designed to conduct the war without disturbing the Southern social system. Radicals and Conservatives agreed in deploring his retention of McClellan in command—an opinion in which most modern military historians concur.

Nor could an informed Northerner see much promise in Lincoln's program for reconstruction, which later historians have so often extolled as a model of statesmanship. A great many congressmen were aware that the President was failing to take into account the inflamed state of passions, North and South, and that he was erroneously presupposing a reasonable, relaxed period of adjustment. It took no great foresight, either, to see that Lincoln was incorrectly assuming that the Southern whites, left to themselves with a minimum of federal guidance, would work out a program to safeguard the rights of the Negroes. To most Northerners, this was like asking the wolves to guarantee the rights of the sheep. Such doubts were, in fact, all too justified, for the reconstruction governments set up by the President did not secure basic justice to the freedmen. . . . The best a public-spirited Northerner could say for Lincoln's reconstruction policy was that, with his political pragmatism, the President refused to be committed inflexibly to any single plan and that perhaps, with time, he might have come to modify his program.

It is not necessary for a historian to agree with these contemporary strictures upon Lincoln the President, but it is important to remember that he was, as J. G. Randall has reminded us, "The Unpopular Mr. Lincoln." Against such a background of uneasy distrust it is easier to understand that the opposition to Lincoln was not a plot by a little band of conspirators in his own party. Instead, virtually all Republicans, whether as Conservative as Thurlow Weed or as Radical as Thaddeus Stevens, were deploring what they considered Lincoln's genial incompetence, his amiable blundering, and his short-sighted want of planning.

Instead of the conventional cliché of a benevolent Lincoln attacked by vindictive Radicals, then, the historian should substitute a complex picture of intraparty feuding, backbiting, and recrimination. The Republican party, it becomes clear, was not truly a national organization during the Civil War years but a coalition of state parties. In many instances these parties were rent by factionalism. The alignment of one faction behind the Lincoln administration and the sending of another into opposition was less a matter of "Conservative" versus "Radical" than of rivalry over power, position, and patronage. In Kansas, for example, the Republican party was distracted by the struggle between Senators S. C. Pomeroy and J. H. Lane. There were no discernible ideological differences between the two men; both were equally vigorous in assailing Lincoln's war policies. But when Pomeroy attached himself to the political fortunes of Secretary Chase, Lane, to bolster his political position in Kansas—and to secure further federal patronage—promptly aligned himself behind the President. Similarly, Maryland was torn by a feud between the Republican Blair family and the Republican Henry Winter Davis. At the outset of the war it was impossible to say which of these was Conservative and which Radical. But when Lincoln chose Montgomery Blair as his postmaster-general, Davis, who had himself desired a cabinet post, was left with no alternative but to assume a strong anti-administration position. In Massachusetts, no small part of Sumner's criticism of Lincoln's foreign policy stemmed from the appointment of his principal Republican enemy, Charles Francis Adams, as minister to Great Britain, an office which Sumner himself desired. . . .

These factional fights were not entirely aimless, however, for behind many of them lay the ancient rivalries between former Whigs and former Democrats. Though recent historians have minimized the significance of party differences in American history, it can be argued that Whigs and Democrats did disagree on such important matters as the powers of the president, the relative strength of the national and state governments, and the relation of the government to the economy. At any rate, it is certain that members of those parties thought they represented differing and opposing principles. The party which elected Abraham Lincoln in 1860 was chiefly an amalgam of these old rival groups, and it was natural that these earlier antagonisms should continue into the war years. Behind the Blair-Davis feud in Maryland, for example, lay the genuine differences between Jacksonian Democrat and Clay Whig. In Illinois, Republicans of Democratic antecedents followed Lyman Trumbull, and those of Whig origins listened to his rival, David Davis. . . . It is at least suggestive that when former-Democrat Chase was attempting to replace Lincoln in 1864 he received his principal support from ex-Democrats now in the Republican party.

This Whig-Democratic tension within the Republican party was especially apparent when the question of restoring the Southern states to the Union was under discussion. The essential problem of reconstruction was to locate dependable Unionists within the South, to whom the future of that section could be safely entrusted. Republicans of Whig origins naturally tended to think of the Southern planters and merchants with whom they had once been allied in the old Whig party. Lincoln's own reconstruction measures were based upon the assumption that this Southern upper class had been coerced into secession and upon the belief that, if encouraged, they would again give conservative leadership to their section. . . . Former Democrats in the Republican party, on the other hand, thought of the great Whig planters as conspirators who had taken their states into secession in order to preserve slavery and consequently looked for real Unionism among their former Democratic political allies, the small farmers of the South. Andrew Johnson's program of excluding wealthy Southerners from leadership in the reconstruction process was a reflection of his Democratic antecedents. Only those thoroughly embittered Republicans like Stevens and Sum-

ner, who saw no Unionism anywhere in the white population of
the South, turned to the Negro as the guarantor of Northern
victory.

This intricate pattern of intraparty Republican rivalries, personal, political, and ideological, offers a truer picture of Civil
War politics than our present oversimplifications about Lincoln
versus the Radicals.

13   *Fawn M. Brodie*
Differences Between Lincoln and the Radicals
Have Been Magnified

Lincoln more than any man of his time felt the full pressure
of the anti-Negro, anti-abolitionist tradition of the Democrats
and Copperheads, which plagued him throughout the war and
rose to formidable proportions during the election of 1864. His
most patient public and private pleadings failed to persuade the
border states to accept gradual emancipation, even with compensation. His Emancipation Proclamation met a mixed reception, a typical border state reaction being that of Representative
Wadsworth of Kentucky, who protested in the House, "As to
that proclamation, we despise and laugh at it. . . . The soldiers
of other States will not execute it. May my curse fall upon
their heads if they do!" A year after the Proclamation Lincoln's
own cabinet member, Montgomery Blair, publicly accused the
"Abolition party" of favoring "amalgamation, equality, and fra-
ternity," and told his Maryland constituents that they would not
lose their slaves. The war was almost over—January 31, 1865—

SOURCE. From Fawn M. Brodie, "Who Defends the Abolitionist?", in *The
Antislavery Vanguard: New Essays on the Abolitionists,* ed. by Martin
Duberman (Copyright © 1965 by Princeton University Press; Princeton
Paperback, 1968), pp. 61–64. Reprinted by permission of Princeton Uni-
versity Press and the editor.

before the Republicans could muster enough votes to pass a
resolution calling for a Thirteenth Amendment prohibiting
slavery and then it passed only with the aid of Lincoln's quiet
backstage pressure. As Thaddeus Stevens commented cryptically,
"The greatest measure of the nineteenth century was passed by
corruption, aided and abetted by the purest man in America."

The sobering story of the Democratic and Copperhead opposition to Lincoln, and the extraordinary persistence of proslavery
sentiment in the North, needs retelling. What we have had instead—as in *Lincoln and the Radicals* by T. Harry Williams—is
a minute examination of the differences between Lincoln and
the abolitionists and Radicals in his own party. To all the crimes
already laid at the feet of the abolitionists a new one was
added—the crime of differing with Lincoln. And though the
actual differences had much to do with timing and very little to
do with principle or compassion, many historians have so
magnified them that they have gravely distorted the image of
Lincoln himself.

Back in 1862 Edward Pollard, writing his *Southern History of
the War,* called Lincoln a "Yankee monster of inhumanity and
falsehood." Now historians from every section and representing
every shade of opinion try desperately to claim him for their
own. But the attempt to turn Lincoln into something close to
an anti-abolitionist would have astonished the old Confederates,
who realistically—from their point of view—labeled Lincoln an
abolitionist despite his public protestations that he was not one at
all but only antislavery. For them it was enough that he was
on public record as "hating" slavery as hoping for its "ultimate
extinction," and resolutely opposing its expansion.

They did not overlook the fact that as early as 1854 he had
said that slavery was "hid away in the constitution, just as an
afflicted man hides away a wen or cancer, which he dares not
cut out at once, lest he bleed to death; with the promise, nevertheless, that the cutting may begin at the end of a given time."
Lincoln had been found of this simile, returning to it often in
the debates with Douglas. No one knows if ever he secretly
fantasied himself as surgeon. But certainly when the war powers
gave him the right to cut, he did not refrain from using the

knife, and his timing and skill were of the highest professional quality.

In our time E. Merton Coulter writes that Lincoln "held out tenaciously against issuing a proclamation freeing the slaves," and Hudson Strode holds that Lincoln "could foresee no bright destiny for Negroes in the United States, and, by his own testimony he wanted them out of the country." David Donald in his *Lincoln Reconsidered* asserts, "On all crucial issues Lincoln was closer to George B. McClellan or Horatio Seymour than to many members of his own party." And Donald reduces the whole abolitionist Zeitgeist to a neurotic disturbance by writing cynically, "The freeing of the slaves ended the great crusade that had brought purpose and joy to the abolitionist. For them Abraham Lincoln was not the Great Emancipator; he was the killer of the dream."

Such statements are bolstered by a dexterous selection of early Lincoln statements and by ignoring the steady evolution of Lincoln's attitude toward Negro rights and the massive evidence of his cooperation with men in the radical wing of his party and they with him. The total Lincoln antislavery record, beginning with his earliest attempts as Congressman to get slavery abolished in the District of Columbia, and continuing to the passage of the Thirteenth Amendment, which he described with satisfaction as "the king's cure for all the evils," and "the great event of the nineteenth century," is as certain a march in the direction of Negro freedom as that of Jefferson Davis and Robert E. Lee was away from it.

The record includes Lincoln's friendship and affection for Radicals like Edwin M. Stanton, Owen Lovejoy, and Charles Sumner, as well as his respect for and sagacious use of the great parliamentary talents of Thaddeus Stevens. It includes Lincoln's approval of Congressional bills providing for abolition of segregation on horsedrawn streetcars in Washington, for the acceptance of Negro witnesses in Federal courts, for the equalizing of penalties for the same crime. It includes his friendship for the famous ex-slave Frederick Douglass, and his easy willingness to break a precedent and accept a Negro as Ambassador from Haiti. It includes his urging of Federal aid for the welfare and schooling of the newly freed slave. In his last public address Lincoln urged *immediate* suffrage for the educated Negro and the Negro soldier. This pointed the way to eventual universal Negro suffrage.

14 *T. Harry Williams*
Shall We Keep the Radicals?

There were . . . in the Republican party during the Civil War men and factions that called themselves Radicals and Conservatives, and they spoke of their beliefs as entities that could be identified and segregated one from the other. Their sense or system of dichotomy has passed into the historical writing about the war. The conflict between the Radicals and the Conservatives, revolving around the wartime disposal to be made of slavery, looms large in all the books, and has been until recently a staple article in all analyses of Northern and Republican politics. But now it has been challenged by some scholars and most notably by Professor David Donald. . . His argument, if I do it justice, runs as follows. Historians have made the Radicals the villains of an illusory struggle. Any president is bound to disappoint most of the people who voted for him, even as many as nine-tenths of them; so Lincoln disappointed his followers, most of whom, regardless of their factional persuasion, viewed him as incompetent or imperfect; Lincoln, like every president, was the center of a tug for power between various groups in his party; he worked with these factions, including the Radicals, and not against them; and in the final analysis Lincoln has no serious differences with the Radicals, who were not a cohesive faction

SOURCE. T. Harry Williams, "Lincoln and the Radicals: An Essay in Civil War History and Historiography," in Grady McWhiney, ed., *Grant, Lee, Lincoln and the Radicals* (Evanston, Illinois: Northwestern University Press, 1964), pp. 93–107, 109, 113–115. Reprinted by permission of the publisher, the editor and the author.

during the war and did not become one until Reconstruction. In short, Mr. Donald seems to be telling us that what we have supposed was an important and unique conflict was only an expression of the normal workings of American politics and that such contests characterize all administrations. Having disposed of the Civil War Radicals, Mr. Donald apparently is content to rest, but others want to push his thesis toward new frontiers. Professor Eric McKitrick, in a recent study of Reconstruction, states that the Radicals were not a particularly cohesive or effective faction even in the years after the war and that they did not control the process of reconstruction. Obviously we are moving toward a new interpretation of the whole Civil War era which will run thus: There were no Radicals and besides they weren't very radical.

This latest view of the Radicals, this revision of revisionism, we may say, reflects in part one of the most settled convictions of historians—that they know more about what the people of a particular time were up to than the people concerned. But in larger measure it is the expression of something more important, of a new style or doctrine in historical thought. In recent years we have been subjected in the literature to what has been called the history of consensus and consent. Influenced by both the insecurities and the conservatism of our age, historians have sought for security and unity in the American past. They have depicted an America which has never been beset by serious differences or divisions, one in which all parties and factions have worked toward essentially the same objectives. . . . There are, however, signs of a reaction against the whole concept of consensus history, and we may be about to experience one of those examinations of contrasting views that impel introspection and clarify the meaning of history. At this budding point in Civil War historiography, when new interpretations that have not entirely crystallized meet old ones that may need modification, it would seem essential to reconsider the issue most in dispute. The question at hand might be phrased: Shall we keep the Radicals? . . .

Any analysis of the Radicals must, of course, begin with some consideration of the Republican party, for the Radicals have to

be related to other elements in the organization and to the organization as a whole. The Republican party was, perhaps because
of its youth, a remarkably homogeneous and tenacious assem-
blage. Agglomerate in make-up, like all our major parties, it
nevertheless displayed a fairly consistent purpose in moving
toward its economic and political objectives. Its cohesiveness
and cunning in the economic area have been exaggerated by historians, but still it was in substantial accord on vital legislation;
certainly it was not rent by any serious economic differences,
and those that arose were susceptible of ready adjustment. Like
all parties, it had a strong institutional urge to survive, to grasp
and hold the power and patronage that meant survival, and this
quality has perhaps not been sufficiently noted by historians.
Because it was new to the ways of office, it was especially avid
to retain the rewards of office, and this desire invested it with a
rare capacity to sustain internal differences and absorb them. . . .

Only one serious divisive issue agitated the party, but this
issue, because of its unique nature and because it tended to pull
other issues into its orbit, was of overruling importance. The
question was, of course, slavery, or more accurately, the policy
to be adopted toward slavery during the war. All factions of the
party were in one degree or another opposed to the peculiar institution and committed to its extinction. But they differed as to
when and how it should be extinguished. To borrow European
terms, on the slavery problem there was a right, a center, and
a left faction. The right was made up mainly of border-state
Unionists, such as Speed, Bates, and Montgomery Blair, who
were antislavery more in theory than in fact, who were more
content to talk against slavery than to act against it, and who
hoped its ultimate extinction would come by state action and
would be fairly ultimate. The center included the men whom we
call, and who called themselves, the Conservative Republicans.
Before the war they had advocated some plan to bring about
the eventual and gradual disappearance of slavery, their favorite device being to prevent it from expanding to the territories
and thus causing it to wither on the vine and die. Once the war
started they were willing to hasten its demise; they thought that
a plan should be devised during the war to accomplish the de-

struction of slavery *after* the war, preferably by a scheme of compensated emancipation. . . . The left comprised the Radicals, who became during the war the dominant faction. The Radicals were more committed to the destruction of slavery than any of the other factions, and they were determined to use the war as an opportunity to strike it down. Put simply and baldly, their program was to destroy slavery as part of the war process, to destroy it suddenly and, if necessary, violently, to destroy it, if not in revenge, with passion.

All factions of the Republican party were united, then, on certain objectives. They were for the Union, they were for the war to preserve it, and they were antislavery. Only on the issue of how to proceed against slavery during the war did they divide seriously and significantly, and this division appeared . . . almost immediately after the conflict began. Lincoln too saw the issue emerging, and he knew what it portended. As if sensing the program the Radicals would soon develop, the President, in his message to Congress of December, 1861, delineated what measures against slavery should not be executed. "In considering the policy to be adopted for suppressing the insurrection," he said, "I have been anxious and careful that the inevitable conflict for this purpose shall not degenerate into a violent and remorseless revolutionary struggle. . . . We should not be in haste to determine that radical and extreme measures, which may reach the loyal as well as the disloyal, are indispensable." Interestingly enough, when toward the end of the war George W. Julian described how the Radicals had wrenched control from the administration and imposed their own policy toward slavery, he used almost exactly Lincoln's own words to characterize the Radical procedure. From the beginning of the war the Radicals had, Julian explained, "persistently urged a vigorous policy, suited to remorseless and revolutionary violence, till the Government felt constrained to embrace it." . . . These are not the kind of terms customarily employed by politicians to characterize the program of other politicians, especially those of the same party; and these are not the kind of labels that American politicians ordinarily accept, let alone boast of wearing. We are dealing here, it is emphasized again, with something decidedly

out of the ordinary in politics. The Civil War is the only
episode in our history, or the only important episode, when men
have insisted on the total or absolute solution to a problem, and
in the North the Radicals were the men with the final solution.
The divisive issue in the Republican party was, therefore, verita-
ble, concrete, substantial, and, above all, abnormal to the political
process.

In attempting to structure the Radicals, it is necessary at
the start to discard any modern concepts of radicalism, notably
those related to an economic basis. The Radicals and other Republicans may have had their differences on particular issues,
but essentially their economic beliefs were fairly conventional.
Nor were the Radicals radical in the European sense of wanting
to make over all at once all of society. But they were radical,
as they realized and, indeed, proudly proclaimed, in one area
of thought and action and on one issue. The area might be narrow but it contained most of the social tensions then occupying
the American people, and the issue might be solitary but at the
time it overrode all others. The Radicals were real radicals in
that they wanted to accomplish a great change in society, or
in one part of it, namely, to destroy slavery and to punish those
who supported slavery. . . .

The broadest characterization to be made of the Radicals,
the one that encompasses practically all their qualities, is that
they were doctrinaire and dogmatic. They possessed truth and
justice and they had the total solution; they were men of principle and they were prepared to enforce their principles. "The
radical men are the men of principle," Ben Wade boasted; "they
are the men who feel what they contend for. They are not your
slippery politicians who can jigger this way or that, or construe
a thing any way to suit the present occasion. They are the men
who go deeply down for principle and are not to be detached by
any of your higgling. The sternness of their principle has revo-
lutionized this whole continent." In short, the Radicals were
not pragmatic or empiric; and not being so, they were not typical
or normal American politicians. They could not conceive that
sometimes the imposition of right principles produces bad results, they could not credit that sometimes the removal of an

evil may cause greater evils; they were so sure of their motives that they did not have to consider results. . . .

Essentially the conflict in the Republican ranks was over how the problem of slavery should be approached, on a basis of principle or pragmatism. This is not to say that all Conservatives were pragmatic. Some were, in their own way, quite as doctrinaire as were most Radicals, but many were not; and the great Conservative and the great opponent of radicalism was the supreme pragmatist in our history. And it was precisely because he was what he was that the Radicals scorned and despised Abraham Lincoln. . . . Historians will, of course, give different readings to the same documents, but it would seem that the personal criticism of Lincoln emanating from the Radicals was of a different order from that coming from other Republicans, being particularly savage and venomous. At any rate, we know that Lincoln was deeply pained by the tone of the Radical blasts, notably by the Wade-Davis Manifesto, and that he once spoke sadly of the "petulant and vicious fretfulness" displayed by most Radicals.

But the Radicals went beyond mere evaluations of Lincoln as an executive or administrator. In their lexicon the theme was that the President was a man without principle or doctrine. He had no antislavery instincts, no crusading zeal to eradicate evil, no blueprint for reform, no grasp of immutable truth. Wendell Phillips, on the eve of the election of 1864, expressed exactly the Radical summation of Lincoln. The note struck by Phillips was not that Lincoln was incompetent or even bad but that being without dogma he was simply nothing. . . . Running all through the Radical literature on Lincoln is a suggestion of condescension, the condescension of the ideologue for the pragmatist, of the generalist for the particularist. . . . Casting up at the end of the war the reasons for the triumph of the Union, L. Maria Child recalled the "want of moral grandeur" in the government during the first years of the war and the consequent failure of Northern arms. But then Radical counsels had come to prevail and immediately things changed: great ideas and great principles were installed and victory had naturally followed. Simple Lincoln had not understood that victory depended on the right doctrine, but he had gone along with the men who did. How fortunate it was after all, Miss Child patronized, that he had been a man who was willing to grow.

The ardent feminine Radical was certain that the hearts of the soldiers had been sad and cold until the correct dogma had been instituted, whereupon they had become irresistible. But in the early stages of the war many Radicals, while they hoped the men in uniform would think right, did not wish them to become too victorious too soon. Rather, they were willing that the armies should fight on indefinitely, until the voters at home were persuaded to the Radical program; and if reverses in the field were necessary to effect this conversion the Radicals were quite content to have the soldiers suffer the reverses. This is not to say that the Radicals wanted the armies or the war to fail. But certainly many of them, in their devotion to doctrine, were prepared to prolong the struggle until their objectives were accomplished. . . . The speeches and writings of Radicals of all sizes are crammed with affirmations that defeat will be good for the popular soul, that penance and punishment must precede redemption. Wendell Phillips intoned: "God grant us so many reverses that the government may learn its duty; God grant us the war may never end till it leaves us on the solid granite of impartial liberty and justice." And from that most doctrinaire of all Radicals, Charles Sumner, came this: "We are too victorious; I fear more from our victories than from our defeats. . . . The God of battles seems latterly to smile upon us. I am content that he should not smile too much. . . . There must be more delay and more suffering,—yet another 'plague' before all will agree to 'let my people go': and the war cannot, must not, end till then." It is contended that such statements do not represent the normal sentiments of politicians discussing normal political issues. They are not oratory but theology. Whatever they reflect of the sincerity and sense of justice of the speakers, they reveal that determination in radicalism and abolitionism to remove evil regardless of who suffered, the sinners in the South and even the drafted instruments who were, at the right time, to crush the sinners. These are the implacable declarations of men who had the absolute solution and who would insist on that solution regardless of consequence. The pragmatist in the White House could not have spoken in such a spirit, nor would he, if he could help it, accept the solution.

As a part of the solution, the Radicals proposed to make over the social structure of the South, to make it over to accord with the dictates of moral theory. This determination is one of the most significant manifestations of their doctrinaire zeal. "The whole social system of the Gulf States is to be taken to pieces," exulted Phillips; "every bit of it." . . . Not only would the Radicals reconstruct the society of a part of the country, but in the process of removing an evil that could not be abided they would punish the people responsible for the evil, punish them not reluctantly or with stern love but with a kind of ecstasy that went with the joy of doing God's will, with a zeal that became men charged with constituting a society that glorified their Creator. The punishment of slaveholders is an element that bulks large in Radical thought. It deserves more attention than it has received from historians as another key to the Radical psychology and as an indicator of the sweep of the Radical program. The Radicals proposed penalties that were not only stringent but remarkably durable.

From the Radical chorus on what should be done to the South a few voices are extracted. Owen Lovejoy: "If there is no other way to quell this rebellion, we will make a solitude, and call it peace." Zachariah Chandler: "A rebel has sacrificed all his rights. He has no right to life, liberty, property, or the pursuit of happiness. Everything you give him, even life itself, is a boon which he has forfeited." Thaddeus Stevens: "Abolition—yes! abolish everything on the face of the earth but this Union; free every slave—slay every traitor—burn every Rebel mansion, if these things be necessary to preserve this temple of freedom to the world and to our posterity." . . .

Again it is submitted that statements such as these are more than the rhetorical mouthings common to politicians, more than the customary commentaries on normal political issues. These are the expressions of abstract reformers who were so certain of their motives that they did not have to consider the results of their course, who were so convinced of their righteousness that they wanted to punish the sinners as well as the sin. One may readily concede that the antislavery cause was a noble endeavor and yet at the same time note, as Lincoln noted, that it had its darker and socially mischievous side. . . .

Historians have talked much about the deep-laid plans of the Radicals to solidify and expand their dominance in the years after the war. The recent revisionists have questioned this thesis, doubting that the Radicals saw that far ahead, and they are in part right. Indeed, on one count the opposite of the conventional view would seem to be true—that in their terrible certainty and zeal the Radicals did not look far enough into the future. Intent on removing a sin, they did not consider, as did the pragmatic Lincoln, that the sinners would have to be lived with after the war. They were for the Union but in it they would make no viable place for the defeated side. Perhaps the real criticism of the Radicals should be not that they planned too well but too little.

The Radicals not only spoke a revolutionary vocabulary, they employed on occasion revolutionary techniques. Somewhere along the line, probably in the long frustrating struggle against slavery, many of them had acquired revolutionary temperaments. To achieve their objectives or just to snap the unbearable tension of being unable to lay hands on evil, that is, slavery, they were willing to use short cuts, to skirt around the edges, to play loosely with accepted procedures; they talked openly of the end justifying the means; they were ruthlessly determined to accomplish their end because it was both theirs and right. We see one aspect of this psychology, and again the constant commitment to doctrine, in the insistent Radical demand that the management of the war, in its civilian and military branches, be entrusted exclusively to Radical antislavery men, to men who, in Radical terminology, had their hearts in the struggle. It may be said by some that the Radicals were only trying in the normal fashion of politicians to get their hands on some patronage. But surely any reading of the documents will demonstrate that this was more than just a grab for jobs. These dedicated doctrinaires intended if they could to proscribe from the government and the armies every individual who did not agree with them completely. The expressions of

Radical opinion on this goal are too plentiful and too plain to admit of much doubt. Over and over they say that the President who did not know doctrine must be surrounded in his cabinet by men of doctrine, that the armies must be led by "generals of ideas" who were swayed by "the great invisible forces," that the imposition of a Radical policy on the administration would be barren unless it was administered by Radical men. . . .

The most instructive demonstration of the revolutionary temperament of the Radicals, certainly for the historian, is their endeavor to establish the primacy of Congress in the governmental system. Here, as with other areas of war politics, it is necessary to lay down some initial qualifications. Some Conservatives advocated a larger role for Congress in the management of the war, and the Radical push in this direction represented in part the normal reaction of the legislative branch against the executive in a time of crisis. But the Radical leaders proposed to go beyond a defense against executive expansion or even an enlargement of legislative influence. Essentially they wanted to set up a kind of Congressional dictatorship. They would do this formally—some Radicals favored the installation of the English cabinet system—or, preferably, informally, by overshadowing the executive with the power of Congress. The latter course was exemplified notably in the creation and the career of the Committee on the Conduct of the War, a unique agency in our history and undeniably a Radical-dominated body. Ostensibly an investigative mechanism, it attempted to be also and with substantial success a policy-forming institution. The Committee's work cannot be adequately treated here, but in summary it is accurate to say that in no other of our conflicts did Congress attain such a dominant voice in the direction of military affairs. . . .

Both of the Republican factions were puzzled at times as to which side Lincoln espoused, and so also were more objective observers. "The conservative Republicans think him too much in the hands of the radicals," one reporter noted, "while the radical Republicans think him too slow, yielding, and half-hearted." A Democratic journalist, trying to analyze the conflict in the Republican party, came closer than he perhaps realized to the truth, to the paradox that the Republicans were at once concurrent and contrary. Lincoln was in his beliefs, thought this man, as one with the Radicals. But he was not accepted by them as a leader because he had not done "everything in their particular way, and at their designated moment." Congressman Owen Lovejoy, a Radical without the personal dislike of Lincoln manifested by many Radicals, propounded an identical analysis in more striking language. The President was like a man trying to handle two horses, Lovejoy conjectured. The superb Radical horse wanted to clear all barriers at once, while the poor Conservative horse held back. Lovejoy criticized Lincoln for checking the forward steed but then added: "If he does not drive as fast as I would, he is on the same road, and it is a question of time." These last two comments embody the essence of the paradox and the essence of the Republican division. Lincoln and the Radicals *were* in agreement on the ultimate goal, the extinction of slavery. On the great end there was no fundamental difference between them. But they *were* divided on the method and the timing, on how fast and in what manner they should move toward the goal. Both were committed to bringing about a wrenching social change. One would do it with the experimental caution of the pragmatist, the other with the headlong rush of the doctrinaire. And this matter of method on this particular issue was a fundamental difference. . . .

Lincoln was on the slavery question, as he was on most matters, a conservative. Unlike the ultra Radicals, he could tolerate evil, especially when he feared that to uproot it would produce greater evils. But he was not the kind of conservative who refused to move at all against evil, who let his pragmatism fade into expediency, who blindly rejected change when it could not be denied. Yet there were just such men among the ultra Conservatives of his party, and Lincoln opposed them as he did the ultra Radicals. He knew that he was not completely with them, and . . . he would not let the Conservatives control the slavery issue. He knew too that he was against the Radicals and also with them. Speaking of the Missouri Radicals but doubtless having the whole genre in mind, he said: "They are utterly lawless—the unhandiest devils in the world to deal with—but after all their faces are set Zionwards." He did work with the Radicals but he also resisted them. He used them—as he did the Conservatives—to effect a great social change with the smallest possible social dislocation. It would indeed be an error . . . to make too much out of the conflict in the Republican party over slavery. It would be a greater error to dismiss this unique episode and its unique issue as something normal or average and to treat it on the level of ordinary politics. There is little about the Civil War that is ordinary.

PART FOUR

Lincoln and the Negro

Lincoln and the Negro

I have been down there to see the President; and as you were not there, perhaps you may like to know how the President of the United States received a black man at the White House. I will tell you how he received me—just as you have seen one gentleman receive another; with a hand and a voice well-balanced between a kind cordiality and a respectful reserve. I tell you I felt big there!

FREDERICK DOUGLASS, 1863

It is impossible to avoid the conclusion that so far as the Negro was concerned, Lincoln could not escape the moral insensitivity that is characteristic of the average white American.

RICHARD HOFSTADTER, 1948

Lincoln was fully aware of the limited moral resources of his party and his section of the country. He knew that there were limits beyond which popular conviction and conscience could not be pushed in his time.

C. VANN WOODWARD, 1958

Lincoln wrote the Emancipation Proclamation amid severe psychological and legal handicaps. Unlike Jefferson, whose Declaration of Independence was a clean break with a legal and constitutional system that had hitherto restricted thought and action, Lincoln was compelled to forge a document of freedom for the slaves within the existing constitutional system and in a manner that would give even greater support to that constitutional system. This required not only courage and daring, but considerable ingenuity as well.

JOHN HOPE FRANKLIN, 1963

Any discussion of Lincoln and the American Negro is ringed with difficulties, not the least of which is the question of whether he should be judged by the standards of his time, or by the standards of our time, or by some absolute standard—or whether he should be judged at all. In addition, it is usually impossible to determine how much personal feeling Lincoln expressed in his statements acknowledging and describing popular feeling about race. Thus, to a deputation of free Negroes, he confessed his inability to change the discriminatory structure of American society but sidestepped the theoretical question of what he would do about it if he could. Even the man's own words can be misleading when quoted, as they so often are, without explanation of their historical context. For instance, his most explicit disavowals of racial equality were made during the debates with Douglas, the one campaign of his life in which he was consistently charged with favoring racial equality and in which the issue seemed likely to be decisive. These statements therefore represent Lincoln's utmost concession to anti-Negro feeling in an effort to win an antislavery victory. In fact, throughout his entire career Lincoln's attitude toward the black race was obscured by his primary concern with the problem of slavery. The Thirteenth Amendment did not pass Congress until January 31, 1865, and was not ratified until many months after Lincoln's death. His repeated advocacy of colonization appears less absurd if it is viewed as a gesture designed to drain off some of the continuing opposition to emancipation. Such an explanation gains credibility when one also reads his comments on the fear that freedmen would "swarm forth and cover the whole land."

After the opening selections from Lincoln's own words on the subject of the Negro, this chapter continues with a revealing contemporary editorial from the London *Times* which illustrates the hostility manifested in some circles even toward the Emancipation Proclamation. Much writing on Lincoln and the Negro is argument in support of a definite thesis or point of view. Dwight L. Dumond, a Midwestern scholar, admires the abolitionists and attempts to demonstrate that Lincoln was one of them at heart. Lerone Bennett, Jr., senior editor of *Ebony,* presents a bitter indictment of Lincoln as a white supremacist in what amounts to a black militant view of the Civil War. In both selections, questionable statements of fact diminish but do not destroy the force of their central arguments. Like Dumond, Harry V. Jaffa holds Lincoln in high esteem, but not as a crypto-abolitionist. A political scientist who is probably the most thorough student of Lincoln's political thought, Jaffa places Lincoln among "the most conservative of antislavery men" and yet concludes that he was indeed the Great Emancipator. The final piece in this chapter is taken from J. G. Randall's notable four-volume study of *Lincoln the President,* completed after his death by Richard N. Current. It describes some of Lincoln's personal relations with Negroes during his occupancy of the White House.

15

His Own Words: A Representative Selection

You know I dislike slavery; and you fully admit the abstract wrong of it. So far there is no cause of difference. But you say that sooner than yield your legal right to the slave—especially at the bidding of those who are not themselves interested, you would see the Union dissolved. I am not aware that *any one* is bidding you to yield that right; very certainly *I* am not. I leave that matter entirely to yourself. I also acknowledge *your* rights and *my* obligations under the constitution, in regard to your slaves. I confess I hate to see the poor creatures hunted down, and caught, and carried back to their stripes, and unrewarded toils; but I bite my lip and keep quiet. In 1841 you and I had together a tedious low-water trip, on a Steam Boat from Louisville to St. Louis. You may remember, as I well do, that from Louisville to the mouth of the Ohio there were, on board, ten or a dozen slaves, shackled together with irons. That sight was a continual torment to me; and I see something like it every time I touch the Ohio, or any other slave-border. It is hardly fair for you to assume, that I have no interest in a thing which has, and continually exercises, the power of making me miserable. You ought rather to appreciate how much the great body of the Northern people do crucify their feelings, in order to maintain their loyalty to the constitution and the Union.

Lincoln to Joshua F. Speed, August 24, 1855

. . . the Chief Justice does not directly assert, but plainly assumes, as a fact, that the public estimate of the black man is more favorable *now* than it was in the days of the Revolution. This assumption is a mistake. In some trifling particulars, the condition of that race has been ameliorated; but, as a whole, in this country, the change between then and now is decidely the other way; and their ultimate destiny has never appeared so hopeless as in the last three or four years. . . . All the powers of earth seem rapidly combining against him. Mammon is after him; ambition follows, and philosophy follows, and the Theology of the day is fast joining the cry. They have him in his prison house; they have searched his person, and left no prying instrument with him. One after another they have closed the heavy iron doors upon him, and now they have him, as it were, bolted in with a lock of a hundred keys, which can never be unlocked without the concurrence of every key; the keys in the hands of a hundred different men, and they scattered to a hundred different and distant places; and they stand musing as to what invention, in all the dominions of mind and matter, can be produced to make the impossibility of his escape more complete than it is.

It is grossly incorrect to say or assume that the public estimate of the negro is more favorable now than it was at the origin of the government.

Speech at Springfield, June 26, 1857

. . . anything that argues me into his idea of perfect social and political equality with the negro, is but a specious and fantastic arrangement of words, by which a man can prove a horse chesnut to be a chesnut horse. . . . I have no purpose to introduce political and social equality between the white and the black races. There is a physical difference between the two, which in my judgment will probably forever forbid their living together upon the footing of perfect equality, and inasmuch as it becomes a necessity that there must be a difference, I, as well as Judge Douglas, am in favor of the race to which I belong, having the superior position. I have never said anything to the contrary, but I hold that notwithstanding all this, there is no reason in the world why the negro is not entitled to all the natural rights enumerated in the Declaration of Independence, the right to life, liberty and the pursuit of happiness. I hold that he is as much entitled to these as the white man. I agree with Judge Douglas he is not my equal in many respects—certainly not in color, perhaps not in moral or intellectual endowment. But in the right to eat the bread, without leave of anybody else, which his own hand earns, he is my equal and the equal of Judge Douglas, and the equal of every living man.

First Lincoln-Douglas Debate, Ottawa, August 21, 1858

If A. can prove, however conclusively, that he may, of right, enslave B.—why may not B. snatch the same argument, and prove equally, that he may enslave A?

You say A. is white, and B. is black. It is *color,* then; the lighter, having the right to enslave the darker? Take care. By this rule, you are to be slave to the first man you meet, with a fairer skin than your own.

You do not mean *color* exactly? You mean the whites are *intellectually* the superiors of the blacks, and therefore have the right to enslave them? Take care again. By this rule, you are to be slave to the first man you meet, with an intellect superior to your own.

But, say you, it is a question of *interest;* and, if you can make it your *interest,* you have the right to enslave another. Very well. And if he can make it his interest, he has the right to enslave you.

Undated fragment, c. 1854–1859

You and we are different races. We have between us a broader difference than exists between almost any other two races. Whether it is right or wrong I need not discuss, but this physical difference is a great disadvantage to us both, as I think your race suffer very greatly, many of them by living among us, while ours suffer from your presence. In a word we suffer on each side. If this is admitted, it affords a reason at least why we should be separated. . . . Your race are suffering, in my judgment, the greatest wrong inflicted on any people. But even when you cease to be slaves, you are yet far removed from being placed on an equality with the white race. You are cut off from many of the advantages which the other race enjoy. The aspiration of men is to enjoy equality with the best when free, but on this broad continent, not a single man of your race is made the equal of a single man of ours. Go where you are treated the best, and the ban is still upon you.

I do not propose to discuss this, but to present it as a fact with which we have to deal. I cannot alter it if I would. It is a fact, about which we all think and feel alike, I and you. We look to our condition, owing to the existence of the two races on this continent. I need not recount to you the effects upon white men, growing out of the institution of slavery. I believe in its general evil effects on the white race. See our present condition—the country engaged in war!—our white men cutting one another's throats, none knowing how far it will extend; and then consider what we know to be the truth. But for your race among us there could not be war, although many men engaged on either side do not care for you one way or the other. Nevertheless, I repeat, without the institution of slavery and the colored race as a basis, the war could not have an existence. It is better for us both, therefore, to be separated.

Remarks on colonization to a deputation of Negroes, August 14, 1862

I cannot make it better known than it already is, that I strongly favor colonization. And yet I wish to say there is an objection urged against free colored persons remaining in the country, which is largely imaginary, if not sometimes malicious.

It is insisted that their presence would injure, and displace white labor and white laborers. If there ever could be a proper time for mere catch arguments, that time surely is not now. In times like the present, men should utter nothing for which they would not willingly be responsible through time and in eternity. Is it true, then, that colored people can displace any more white labor, by being free, than by remaining slaves? If they stay in their old places, they jostle no white laborers; if they leave their old places, they leave them open to white laborers. Logically, there is neither more nor less of it. . . .

But it is dreaded that the freed people will swarm forth, and cover the whole land? Are they not already in the land? Will liberation make them any more numerous? Equally distributed among the whites of the whole country, and there would be but one colored to seven whites. Could the one, in any way, greatly disturb the seven? There are many communities now, having more than one free colored person to seven whites; and this, without any apparent consciousness of evil from it.

Annual Message to Congress, December 1, 1862

The emancipation proclamation applies to Arkansas. I think it is valid in law, and will be so held by the courts. I think I shall not retract or repudiate it. Those who shall have tasted actual freedom I believe can never be slaves, or quasi slaves again.

Lincoln to Stephen A. Hurlbut, July 31, 1863

You say you will not fight to free negroes. Some of them seem willing to fight for you; but, no matter. Fight you, then, exclusively to save the Union. I issued the proclamation on purpose to aid you in saving the Union. . . . But negroes, like other people, act upon motives. Why should they do any thing for us, if we will do nothing for them? If they stake their lives for us, they must be prompted by the strongest motive—even the promise of freedom. And the promise being made, must be kept.

Lincoln to James C. Conkling, August 26, 1863

Of those who were slaves at the beginning of the rebellion, full one hundred thousand are now in the United States military service, about one-half of which number actually bear arms in the ranks; thus giving the double advantage of taking so much labor from the insurgent cause, and supplying the places which otherwise must be filled with so many white men. So far as tested, it is difficult to say they are not as good soldiers as any.

Annual Message to Congress, December 8, 1863

At the beginning of the war, and for some time, the use of colored troops was not contemplated; and how the change of purpose was wrought, I will not now take time to explain. Upon clear conviction of duty I resolved to turn that element of strength to account; and I am responsible for it to the American people, to the christian world, to history, and on my final account to God. Having determined to use the negro as a soldier, there is no way but to give him all the protection given to any other soldier.

Speech at Sanitary Fair in Baltimore, April 18, 1864

I repeat the declaration made a year ago, that "while I remain in my present position I shall not attempt to retract or modify the emancipation proclamation, nor shall I return to slavery any person who is free by the terms of that proclamation, or by any of the Acts of Congress." If the people should, by whatever mode or means, make it an Executive duty to re-enslave such persons, another, and not I, must be their instrument to perform it.

Annual Message to Congress, December 6, 1864

The amount of constituency, so to speak, on which the new Louisiana government rests, would be more satisfactory to all, if it contained fifty, thirty, or even twenty thousand, instead of only about twelve thousand, as it does. It is also unsatisfactory to some that the elective franchise is not given to the colored man. I would myself prefer that it were now conferred on the very intelligent, and on those who serve our cause as soldiers.

Last public address, April 11, 1865

16   *A Sort of Moral American Pope*

It is rarely that a man can be found to balance accurately mischief to another against advantage to himself. President Lincoln is, as the world says, a good-tempered man, neither better nor worse than the mass of his kind—neither a fool nor a sage, neither a villain nor a saint, but a piece of that common useful clay out of which it delights the American democracy to make great Republican personages. Yet President Lincoln has declared that from the 1st of January next to come every State that is in rebellion shall be in the eye of Mr. Lincoln a Free State. After that date Mr. Lincoln purposes to enact that every slave in a rebel State shall be for ever after free, and he promises that neither he, nor his army, nor his navy will do anything to repress any efforts which the negroes in such rebel States may make for the recovery of their freedom. This means, of course, that Mr. Lincoln will, on the 1st of next January, do his best to excite a servile war in the States which he cannot occupy with his arms. He will run up the rivers in his gunboats; he will seek out the places which are left but slightly guarded, and where the women and children have been trusted to the fidelity of coloured domestics. He will appeal to the black blood of the African; he will whisper of the pleasures of spoil and of the gratification of yet fiercer instincts; and when blood begins to flow and shrieks come piercing through the darkness, Mr. Lincoln will wait till the rising flames tell that all is consummated, and then he will rub his hands and think that revenge is sweet. This is what Mr. Lincoln avows before the world that he is about to do. Now, we are in Europe thoroughly convinced that the death of slavery must follow as necessarily upon the success of the Confederates in this war as the dispersion of darkness occurs upon the rising of the sun; but sudden and forcible emancipation resulting from "the efforts the negroes may make for their actual freedom"

SOURCE. *The Times* (London), October 7, 1862.

can only be effected by massacre and utter destruction. Mr. Lincoln avows, therefore, that he proposes to excite the negroes of the Southern plantations to murder the families of their masters while these are engaged in the war. The conception of such a crime is horrible . . . . even Mr. Lincoln's own recent achievements of burning by gunboats the defenceless villages on the Mississippi are dwarfed by this gigantic wickedness. . . .

Where he has no power Mr. Lincoln will set the negroes free; where he regains power he will consider them as slaves. "Come to me," he cries to the insurgent planters, "and I will preserve your rights as slaveholders; but set me still at defiance, and I will wrap myself in virtue and take the sword of freedom in my hand, and, instead of aiding you to oppress, I will champion the rights of humanity. Here are whips for you who are loyal; go forth and flog or sell your black chattels as you please. Here are torches and knives for employment against you who are disloyal; I will press them into every black hand, and teach their use." Little Delaware, with her 2,000 slaves, shall still be protected in her loyal tyranny. Maryland, with her 90,000 slaves, shall "freely accept or freely reject" any project for either gradual or immediate abolition; but if Mississippi and South Carolina, where the slaves rather outnumber the masters, do not repent, and receive from Mr. Lincoln a licence to trade in human flesh, that human flesh shall be adopted by Mr. Lincoln as the agent of his vengeance. The position is peculiar for a mere layman. Mr. Lincoln, by this proclamation, constitutes himself a sort of moral American Pope. He claims to sell indulgences to [his] own votaries, and he offers them with full hands to all who will fall down and worship him. It is his to bind, and it is his to loose. His decree of emancipation is to go into remote States, where his temporal power cannot be made manifest, and where no stars and stripes are to be seen; and in those distant swamps he is, by a sort of Yankee excommunication, to lay the land under a slavery interdict.

What will the South think of this? The South will answer with a hiss of scorn. But what will the North think of it? What will Pennsylvania say—Pennsylvania, which is already unquiet under the loss of her best customers, and not easy under the absolute despotism of the present Government at Washington? What Boston may say or think is not, perhaps, of much consequence. But what will New York say? It would not answer the purpose of any of these cities to have the South made a howling wilderness. They want the handling of the millions which are produced by the labour of the black man. Pennsylvania desires to sell her manufactures in the South; New York wishes to be again broker, banker, and merchant to the South. This is what the Union means to these cities. They would rather have a live independent State to deal with than a dead dependency where nothing could be earnt. To these practical persons President Lincoln would be, after his black revolution had succeeded, like a dogstealer who should present the anxious owner with the head of his favourite pointer. They want the useful creature alive. The South without its cotton and its sugar and its tobacco would be of small use to New York, or even to Philadelphia; and the South without the produce of its rice and cotton, and its sugar and tobacco, would be but a sorry gain, even if it could be obtained. If President Lincoln wants such a conquest as this, the North is, perhaps, yet strong enough to conquer Hayti. A few fanatics, of course, will shout, but we cannot think that, except in utter desperation and vindictiveness, any real party in the North will applaud this nefarious resolution to light up a servile war in the distant homesteads of the South.

As a proof of what the leaders of the North, in their passion and their despair, would do if they could, this is a very sad document. As a proof of the hopelessness and recklessness which prompt their actions, it is a very instructive document. But it is not a formidable document. We gather from it that Mr. Lincoln has lost all hope of preserving the Union, and is now willing to let any quack try his nostrum. As an act of policy it is, if possible, more contemptible than it is wicked. It may possibly produce some partial risings, for let any armed power publish an exhortation to the labouring class of any community to plunder and murder, and there will be some response. It might happen in London, or Paris, or New York. That Mr. Lincoln's emancipation decrees will have any general effect bearing upon the issue of the war we do not, however, believe. The negroes have already abundantly discovered that the ter der mercies of the Northerners are cruelties. The freedom which is associated with labour in the trenches, military discipline, and frank avowals of personal abhorrence momentarily repeated does not commend itself to the negro nature. . . . We do not think that even now, when Mr. Lincoln plays his last card, it will prove to be a trump. Powerful malignity is a dreadful reality, but impotent malignity is apt to be a very contemptible spectacle. Here is a would-be conqueror and a would-be extirpator who is not quite safe in his seat of government. . . Here is a President who . . . is trembling for the very ground on which he stands. Yet, if we judged only by his pompous proclamations, we should believe that he had a garrison in every city of the South. This is more like a Chinaman beating his two swords together to frighten his enemy than like an earnest man pressing on his cause in steadfastness and truth.

17   *Dwight Lowell Dumond*
          Virtually an Abolitionist

There are historians who hold that Lincoln was not an uncompromising foe of the peculiar institutions of the South; that he had never, before assuming the presidency, proposed or pretended to have a solution for the slavery problem; but, instead, admitted his utter inability, if endowed with complete authority in the matter, to offer such a solution; that the circumstances of war and the passions it loosed forced him to face the slavery problem more boldly; that he turned to the stern doctrine of the emancipation proclamation only after unsuccessfully trying compensated emancipation in the border states, and never abandoned

SOURCE. Dwight Lowell Dumond, *Antislavery Origins of the Civil War in the United States* (Ann Arbor: The University of Michigan Press, 1939), pp. 106–114. Reprinted by permission of the publisher.

hope of effecting some arrangement that might deal more gently and generously with Southern property rights in slaves.

I am constrained to the belief that they are wrong on all these points; that, if Weld and Birney were abolitionists, Lincoln was one; and if they had a plan, he had a better one. Leaving out of consideration every statement reputed to him about which there is the slightest doubt, we still find that he was thoroughly sound on the fundamental principles of abolition doctrine: that the subject of slavery was not a domestic concern of the Southern states, that it was a moral and political evil which menaced the rights of free men, was contrary to the principles enunciated in the Declaration of Independence and a violation of eternal principles of right.

On the question of slavery in its relation to the nonslaveholder we find one significant idea running through all his public pronouncements of the forties and fifties, variously stated according to the exigencies of the occasion, but never retracted: that slavery was hostile to the interests of the poor man, who invariably sought to escape to the free states or to the territories; and that the territories should be kept free by the nation as a haven for the poor. Furthermore, while disclaiming all idea of perfect equality between the races, he did insist over and over, and in unmistakable terms, that the Negro should be free to develop whatever talents he might possess and be protected in his civil right to the enjoyment of the fruits of his own labor. When the Wilmot Proviso was being discussed in Congress, Lincoln was the only Whig member from Illinois, and he voted for it in one form or another not fewer than forty times. He denounced the Dred Scott decision, and said he would not vote for the admission of another slave state. It is true that, as an aspirant for the Senate seat of Douglas, he said that, much as he hated slavery, he would vote to extend it rather than see the Union dissolved, but two years later, as president-elect, he ordered his party in Congress to "hold fast as with chains of steel" on the territorial question, and refused to endorse a compromise on the basis of restoration of the Missouri Compromise line. His reason for this was not limited to his desire to keep the territories free, but embraced the abolition objective of killing the institution in the slave states by circumscription. . . .

What was his attitude toward the fugitive-slave question? In public and as an aspirant for office he avoided the subject as much as possible. In a private letter to Joshua Speed of Kentucky he wrote: "I confess I hate to see the poor creatures hunted down and caught and carried back to their stripes and unrequited toil; but I bite my lips and keep quiet." Yet in his inaugural, speaking to the nation for the first time, did he urge obedience to the fugtive-slave law and provisions for its more effective enforcement by the repeal of the personal-liberty laws? Not at all. He proposed that the existing fugitive-slave law should be repealed and another be substituted guaranteeing the right of habeas corpus and jury trial to the fugitive, thus advocating what would at one stroke quiet all agitation in the North by effectually providing that no fugitives would ever again be returned. The abolitionists had tried to do this by state law until the Supreme Court decision in *Prigg* v. *Pennsylvania* declared Congressional control to be exclusive; and had then turned to personal-liberty laws of doubtful constitutionality. Now that the antislavery forces were coming into control of the federal government, at the first opportunity Lincoln suggested the full use of their new power to settle the question to their complete satisfaction. . . .

Finally, there is the question of emancipation. The great leaders among the abolitionists, those who, in the beginning, knew intimately both the North and the South, never had the least expectation that slavery would be peaceably or voluntarily abolished. . . .

Lincoln expressed the same sentiments in a letter to George Robertson of Kentucky, saying, in effect, that slavery could not be abolished without war: "Since then [1820] experience had demonstrated, I think, that there is no peaceful extinction of slavery in prospect for us. . . . So far as peaceful voluntary emancipation is concerned, the condition of the negro slave in America . . . is now as fixed and hopeless of change for the better, as that of the lost souls of the finally impenitent. The autocrat of all the Russias will resign his crown and proclaim his subjects free republicans sooner than will our American masters voluntarily give up their slaves."

Within one week after his inaugural address, without the knowledge of even his cabinet, he ordered troops into Fort Pickens with the certain knowledge that war would follow, and remarkably soon, considering the tremendous administrative burdens, he proposed compensated emancipation in the District of Columbia and in the border states, but supported by arguments so distinctly foreign to Lincoln's clarity of thought that it is difficult to believe them sincere or made with any hope of endorsement. Lincoln knew, as everyone else did, that the antislavery men had, from the day agitation began, scorned all discussion of compensated emancipation or plans for colonization. These principles were as fundamental and deeply rooted in antislavery doctrine as the sin of slavery itself. Lincoln was one of the shrewdest interpreters of public opinion we have ever had in public life. In his ability to analyze difficult situations he has never been surpassed. As a leader of men he stands alone. In proposing compensated emancipation and colonization he was proposing something he must have known was not acceptable to the Northern people. He was paving the way for— easing the shock of—his Emancipation Proclamation, already formulated in his mind many months before.

From first to last, throughout his entire career, Lincoln was in advance of other public men and of the majority of the people on the slavery issue. On the questions of fugitive slaves, the Dred Scott decision, slavery in the territories, and the exclusion of any more slave states he was thoroughly sound. His Washington Birthday address stamps him as almost a pioneer abolitionist. His "House Divided" speech was delivered six months before Seward's "Irrepressible Conflict" speech and over the protest of his friends. He went to Washington with the Chicago Platform as his gospel and war against the South, the shibboleth of the extremists, as a determined policy. In his Indianapolis speech and his inaugural address, knowing that his every expression would be carefully weighed by millions of men anxious to find in his remarks something to indicate his future policy, he enunciated a political philosophy designed to make the mandates of an unrestrained numerical majority the operative law—it was a complete endorsement of the doctrine of the higher law. And, finally, he did nothing to prevent, if indeed he did not actually precipitate, the war which abolitionists had long hailed as the necessary *modus vivendi* for direct action against slavery.

It is unfortunate that, because he did not hate slaveholders, historians should conclude that he did not hate slavery; and that, because he emphasized the preservation of the Union, emancipation was forced upon him as a means to that end.

The circumstances of Lincoln's early life gave him incomparable human compassion. Few characters are so deeply enshrined in the hearts of so many people; none loved their fellow men more generously than he. For four years he prosecuted the war vigorously, careless of constitutional restraints, but tempering arbitrary action with mercy, and solving as many problems with his heart as with his head, refusing to allow the nation, the heritage of coming generations, to be destroyed by the pride of its enemies or the blunders of its friends, ever mindful of the futility of victory without peace.

We see him, in the last days of the war, standing upon the steps of the Capitol as the armies of Grant and Sherman were closing in a vise the remnant of Lee's gallant army of Virginia. Tall, gaunt, stalwart, with the agony of years finding expression in the deep lines which furrowed his cheeks, but with the inspiration of a great soul suppressing the distress of unbelievable sorrow, speaking his last inaugural:

"Fondly do we hope, fervently do we pray, that this scourge of war may speedily pass away. Yet if God wills that it continue until all the wealth piled by the bondsman's two hundred years of unrequited toil shall be sunk, and until every drop drawn with the lash shall be paid by another drawn with the sword, as was said two thousand years ago, still must it be said that the judgments of the Lord are true and righteous altogether."

Who does not believe he leaned as heavily upon divine providence as the early abolitionists has read those lines to no purpose. His love for the Union was great, but that it was as impelling as his hatred of slavery I cannot believe; and that those who elected him to office were satisfied of his soundness on both points I am firmly convinced.

18 *Lerone Bennett, Jr.*
Lincoln, a White Supremacist

Abraham Lincoln was *not* the Great Emancipator. As we shall see, there is abundant evidence to indicate that the Emancipation Proclamation was not what people think it is and that Lincoln issued it with extreme misgivings and reservations. Even more decisive is the fact that the real Lincoln was a tragically flawed figure who shared the racial prejudices of most of his white contemporaries.

If, despite the record, Lincoln has been misunderstood and misinterpreted, it is not his fault. A conservative Illinois lawyer, cautious and conventional in social matters, Lincoln never pretended to be a racial liberal or a social innovator. He said repeatedly, in public and in private, that he was a firm believer in white supremacy. And his acts supported his assertions. Not only that: Lincoln had profound doubts about the possibility of realizing the rhetoric of the Declaration of Independence and the Gettysburg Address on this soil; and he believed until his death that black people and white people would be much better off separated—preferably with the Atlantic Ocean or some other large and deep body of water between them.

The man's character, his way with words, and his assassination, together with the psychological needs of a racist society, have obscured these contradictions under a mountain of myths which undoubtedly would have amused Lincoln, who had a wonderful sense of the ironic and ridiculous. The myth-makers have not only buried the real Lincoln; they have also managed to prove him wrong. He said once that it was impossible to fool all of the people all of the time. But his apotheosis clearly proves that it is possible to fool enough of them long enough to make a conservative white supremacist a national symbol of racial tolerance and understanding.

SOURCE. Lerone Bennett, Jr., "Was Abe Lincoln a White Supremacist?" in *Ebony* (February 1968), pp. 35–38, 40, 42. Reprinted by permission of the Johnson Publishing Company, Inc.

If the Lincoln myths were the harmless fantasies of children at play, it would be possible to ignore them. But when the myths of children become adult daydreams and when the daydreams are used to obscure deep social problems and to hide historical reality, it becomes a social duty to confront them. . . .

Because . . . we are environed by dangers and because we need all the light we can get; because Abraham Lincoln is not the light, because he is in fact standing in the light, hiding our way; because a real emancipation proclamation has become a matter of national survival and *because no one has ever issued such a document in this country*—because, finally, lies enslave and because the truth is always seemly and proper, it has become urgently necessary to reevaluate the Lincoln mythology. The need for such a reevaluation has already been recognized in some scholarly circles. Some scholars have confronted the ambiguities of the Emancipation Proclamation and have suggested that Lincoln's reputation would be more securely based if it were grounded not on that document but on his services as leader of the victorious North. Analyzing the same evidence, David Donald said in *Lincoln Reconsidered* that perhaps "the secret of Lincoln's continuing vogue is his essential ambiguity. He can be cited on all sides of all questions." Donald was not quite correct, for Lincoln cannot be cited on the side of equal rights for black people, a fact that has discomfited more than one Lincoln Day orator. Commenting on Lincoln's determined opposition to a policy of emancipation, Professor Kenneth Stampp wrote: "Indeed, it may be said that if it was Lincoln's destiny to go down in history as the Great Emancipator, rarely has a man embraced his destiny with greater reluctance than he."

To understand Lincoln's reluctance and his painful ambivalence on the question of race, one must see him first against the background of his times. Born into a poor white family in the slave state of Kentucky and raised in the anti-black environments of southern Indiana and Illinois, Lincoln was exposed from the very beginning to racism.

It would have been difficult, if not impossible, for young Abraham Lincoln to emerge unscathed from this environment. By an immense effort of transcendence, worthy of admiration and long thought, Lincoln managed to free himself of most of the crudities of his early environment. But he did not—and perhaps could not—rise above the racism that was staining the tissue of the nation's soul.

It appears from the record that Lincoln readily absorbed the Negro stereotypes of his environment, for he ever afterwards remained fond of Negro dialect jokes, blackface minstrels and Negro ditties. "Like most white men," Professor Benjamin Quarles wrote, "Lincoln regarded the Negro as such as funny." More to the point, Lincoln, as Quarles also noted, regarded the Negro as inferior. . . .

In the general literature, Lincoln is depicted as an eloquent and flaming idealist, whaling away at the demon of slavery. This view is almost totally false. In the first place, Lincoln was an opportunist, not an idealist. He was a man of the fence, a man of the middle, a man who stated the principle with great eloquence but almost always shied away from rigid commitments to practice. Contrary to reports, Lincoln was no social revolutionary. As a matter of fact, he was an archetypal example of the cautious politician who assails the extremists on both sides. It is not for nothing that cautious politicians sing his praises.

It should be noted, secondly, that Lincoln's position on slavery has been grossly misrepresented. Lincoln was not opposed to slavery; he was opposed to the *extension* of slavery. More than that: Lincoln was opposed to the extension of slavery out of devotion to the interests of white poeple, not out of compassion for suffering blacks. To be sure, he did say from time to time that slavery was "a monstrous injustice." But he also said, repeatedly, that he was not prepared to do anything to remove that injustice where it existed. On the contrary, he said that it was his duty to tolerate and, if necessary, to give practical support to an evil supported by the U.S. Constitution.

More damaging is the fact that Lincoln apparently believed that immediate and general emancipation would be a greater evil than slavery itself. Eulogizing Henry Clay on July 6, 1852, he associated himself with that slaveowner's colonization ideas and said that Clay "did not perceive, as I think no wise man has perceived, how it [slavery] could be at *once* eradicated, without producing a greater evil, even to the cause of human liberty itself." In other speeches of the same period, Lincoln commended travel to black people and noted with admiration that "the children of Israel . . . went out of Egyptian bondage in a body."

A third point of significance is that Lincoln's opposition to the extension of slavery was a late and anomalous growth. In the 1830s and 1840s, in the midst of one of the greatest moral crises in the history of America, Lincoln remained silent and lamentably inactive. In his few public utterances on the subject in the 30s and 40s, he very carefully denounced both slavery and the opponents of slavery. . . .

The Lincoln years in Illinois were years of oppression and reaction. Black people could not vote, testify against white people in court or attend public schools. It was a crime for free black people to settle in the state. Although Lincoln was a powerful figure in state politics for more than a quarter of a century, he made no audible protest against this state of affairs. In fact, he said he preferred it that way. When H. Ford Douglas, a militant black leader, asked Lincoln to support a movement to repeal the law banning black testimony, Lincoln refused.

In the famous series of debates with Stephen Douglas, Lincoln made his position crystal clear. He was opposed, he said, to Negro citizenship and to "the niggers and the white people marrying together." Speaking at Charleston, Illinois, on September 18, 1858, Lincoln said: "I will say, then, that I am not, nor ever have been, in favor of bringing about in any way the social and political equality of the white and black races; (applause) that I am not, nor ever have been, in favor of making voters or jurors of Negroes, nor of qualifying them to hold office, nor to intermarry with white people; and I will say, in addition, to this, that there is a physical difference between the white and black races which I believe will forever forbid the two races living together on terms of social and political equality. And inasmuch as they cannot so live, while they do remain together there must be the position of superior and inferior, and I as much as any other man am in favor of having the superior position assigned to the white race."

Lincoln grew during the war—but he didn't grow much. On every issue relating to the black man—on emancipation, confiscation of rebel land and the use of black soldiers—he was the very essence of the white supremacist with good intentions. In fact, Lincoln distinguished himself as President by sustained and consistent opposition to the fundamental principle of the Proclamation that guaranteed his immortality. Incredible as it may seem now, the man who would go down in history as the Great Emancipator spent the first 18 months of his administration in a desperate and rather pathetic attempt to save slavery where it existed. He began his Presidential career by saying that he had neither the power nor the desire to interfere with slavery in the states. And he endorsed a proposed Thirteenth Amendment which would have guaranteed that slavery would never be molested in existing states and Washington, D.C. . . .

In accordance with the real policy of the Lincoln Administration, the War Department refused to accept black troops and Union generals vied with each other in proving their fealty to slavery. Some generals returned fugitive slaves to rebel owners; others said that if black slaves staged an uprising behind enemy lines they would stop fighting the enemy and turn their fire on their black friends. Union officers who refused to go along with the "soft-on-slavery" policy were court-martialed and cashiered out of the service. When, in August, 1861, General John C. Fremont emancipated Missouri slaves, Lincoln angrily countermanded the proclamation, telling Fremont's wife that "General Fremont should not have dragged the Negro into it. . ." A year later, when General David Hunter freed the slaves in three Southern states, Lincoln again countermanded the order, saying that emancipation was a Presidential function.

That this policy was changed at all was due not to Lincoln's humanitarianism but to rebel battlefield brilliance and the compassion and perservance of a small band of Radical Republicans. Foremost among these men were Charles Sumner, the U.S. senator from Massachusetts; Wendell Phillips, the brilliant agitator from Boston; Frederick Douglass, the bearded black aboltionist; and Thaddeus Stevens, the Pennsylvania congressman who virtually supplanted Abraham Lincoln as the leader of the Republican party. As the war continued and as Northern casualties amounted, the Radical Republicans put events to use and mobilized a public pressure Lincoln could not ignore. Delegation after delegation waited on the President and demanded that he hit the South where it would hurt most by freeing the slaves and arming them. Lincoln parried the pressure with heat and conviction, citing constitutional, political and military reasons to justify his anti-emancipation stand. Lincoln usually expressed his opposition to emancipation in a troubled but polite tone. But he could be pushed across the border of politeness. When Edward L. Pierce urged the President to adopt a more enlightened policy, Lincoln, according to Pierce, exploded and denounced "the itching to get niggers into our lives."

The traditional image of Lincoln is of a harried and large-hearted man fending off "extremists of the left and right" only to emerge at the precise psychological moment to do what he had always wanted to do. This image clashes, unfortunately, with evidence which suggests that sudden and general emancipation was never Lincoln's policy.

Lincoln was given to saying that his constitutional duties prevented him from doing anything substantial to give point to his "oft-expressed *personal* wish that all men everywhere could be free." But it is obvious from the evidence that Lincoln's problems were deeper than that. For when his duty was clear, he refused to act. On several occasions he refused to take anti-slavery action which was mandated by Congress and he sabotaged some anti-slavery legislation by executive inaction. Somehow, duty, in Lincoln's view, almost always worked against the black man.

Lincoln defenders say that he resisted emancipation pressures because of his fear that premature action would alienate white supporters in Northern and Border States and endanger the prosecution of the war. But this view does not come to grips with the fact that Lincoln was *personally* opposed to sudden and general emancipation before 1861 and the further fact that he continued to oppose sudden and general emancipation after the circulating Proclamation proved that his fears were groundless.

Nor does the traditional Lincoln apologia touch the mass of evidence—in Lincoln letters as well as in private and public statements—which shows that Lincoln was personally opposed to sudden emancipation on social and racial grounds.

It was not the fear of emancipation but the fear of what would happen afterwards that palsied Lincoln's hands. He was deeply disturbed by the implications of turning loose four million black people in a land he considered the peculiar preserve of the white man. He spoke often of "the evils of sudden derangement" and warned Congress against "the vagrant destitution which must largely attend immediate emancipation in localities where their numbers are very great." . . .

Lincoln also feared racial conflict. Like many white liberals, he was consumed by fears of black violence. More than one visitor to the White House found him in agony over the possibility of a Nat Turner-like uprising behind the enemy's lines.

An additional factor in Lincoln's opposition to the principle of sudden emancipation was his racial bias. He considered black people unassimilable aliens. There was not, in his view, enough room in America for black and white people. He didn't believe white people would sanction equal rights for black people and he didn't ask white people to sanction equal rights for black people. Since he did not propose to confront racism, he told black people that they would have to travel or accept a subordinate position in American life.

Insofar as it can be said that Lincoln had an emancipation policy, it was to rid America of slaves and Negroes. When he failed in his attempt to end the war without touching slavery, he fell back to a second plan of gradual and compensated emancipation extending over a 37-year-period. This was linked in his thinking with a companion policy of colonizing black people in South America or Africa. . . .

Although Lincoln's plan received a generally hostile reception in the black community, he pursued it with passion and conviction. For several months after the signing of the Emancipation Proclamation, he was deeply involved in a disastrously abortive attempt to settle black people on an island off the coast of Haiti.

When that venture failed, he shifted to the Southwest, conferring with contractors on the feasibility of settling black people in the state of Texas.

While Lincoln was trying to send black people away, Congress was busy emancipating. In the spring and summer of 1862, Congress forbade military officers to return fugitive slaves, authorized the President to accept black soldiers, and emancipated the slaves in Washington, D. C. Finally, on July 17, 1862, Congress passed the Second Confiscation Act, which freed the slaves of all rebels. This act, which has received insufficient attention in general media, was actually more sweeping than the preliminary Emancipation Proclamation, which came two months later.

Lincoln followed Congress' lead slowly and grudgingly, signing most of these acts with evident displeasure. But the drift of events was unmistakable, and Lincoln changed steps, saying with great honesty that he had not controlled events but had been controlled by them. Conferring with the member of a congressional committee charged with drafting a plan for buying the slaves and sending them away, Lincoln urged speed, saying: "You had better come to an agreement. Niggers will never be cheaper."

Orthography apart, Lincoln caught here the spirit of the times. At that moment, in late July of 1862, the Union war effort was bogged down in the marshes of Virginia, and England and France were on the verge of intervening on the side of the Confederacy. At home, the heat was rising fast, fueled by mounting Northern casualties. Faced with mushrooming pressures at home and abroad, Lincoln reversed his course and "conditionally determined," to use his words, to touch the institution of slavery. . . .

Responding to a parallelogram of pressures, Lincoln issued a preliminary Emancipation Proclamation on September 22, 1862. In this document, he warned the South that he would issue a final Emancipation Proclamation in 100 days if the rebellion had not ended by that time. The proclamation outlined a future policy of emancipation, but Lincoln had no joy in the black harvest. To a group of serenaders, who congratulated him on the new policy, Lincoln said: "I can only trust in God I have made no mistake." To his old friend, Joshua F. Speed, Lincoln expressed misgivings and said he had "been anxious to avoid it." To Congressman John Covode of Pennsylvania, Lincoln explained that he had been *"driven to it,"* adding: "But although my duty is plain, it is in some respects painful. . . ." Still another visitor, Edward Stanly, received a dramatic account of Lincoln's resistance to a policy of emancipation. "Mr. Lincoln said," according to Stanly, "that he had prayed to the Almighty to save him from this necessity, adopting the very language of our Saviour, 'If it be possible, let this cup pass from me,' but the prayer had not been answered."

On Thursday, January 1, 1863, Lincoln drank from the cup, and apparently he liked neither the flavor nor the color of the draught. When he started to sign the document, his arm trembled so violently, an eyewitness said, that he could not hold the pen. Lincoln, who was very superstitious, paused, startled. Then, attributing his shakes to hours of hand-shaking at a New Year's Day reception, he scrawled his name, saying he did not want the signature to be "tremulous" because people would say "he had some compunctions."

He had "compunctions."

Nothing indicates this better than the Emancipation Proclamation which is, as J. G. Randall and Richard N. Current indicated, "more often admired than read." Cold, forbidding, with all the moral grandeur of a real estate deed, the Proclamation does not enumerate a single principle hostile to slavery and it contains not one quotable sentence. As a document, it lends weight to the observation of Lincoln's law partner, William Herndon, who wrote: "When he freed the slaves, there was no heart in the act."

There wasn't much else in it, either. Rightly speaking, the Emancipation Proclamation, as Ralph Korngold wrote, was "not an Emancipation Proclamation at all." The document was drafted in such a way that it freed few, if any, slaves. It did not apply to slaves in the Border States and areas under federal control in the South. In other words, Lincoln "freed" slaves where he had no power and left them in chains where he had power. The theory behind the Proclamation, an English paper noted, "is not that a human being cannot justly own another, but that he cannot own him unless he is loyal to the United States."

The Proclamation argues so powerfully against itself that some scholars have suggested that Lincoln was trying to do the opposite of what he said he was doing. In other words, the suggestion is that the Emancipation Proclamation was a political stratagem by which Lincoln hoped to outflank the Radicals, buy time, and forestall a definitive act of emancipation. This is not the place to review the political stratagem theory in detail. Suffice it to say that on the basis of the evidence one can make a powerful case for the view that Lincoln never intended to free the slaves, certainly not immediately.

To this bleak picture one should add in all justice that Lincoln can be quoted on both sides of the issue. He reportedly said later that the Proclamation and the arming of black soldiers constituted the heaviest blows against the rebellion. It should also be said that Lincoln, after a period of vacillation and doubt, helped to win passage of the Thirteenth Amendment, which made the paper freedom of the Proclamation real. Having said that, it remains to be said that Lincoln never fully accepted the fundamental principle of the Proclamation and the Thirteenth Amendment. As late as February, 1865, he was still equivocating on the issue of immediate emancipation. At an abortive peace conference with Confederate leaders at Hampton Roads, Virginia, Lincoln said, according to Alexander Stephens, that he had never been in favor of immediate emancipation, even by the states. He spoke of the "many evils attending" immediate emancipation and suggested, as he had suggested on other occasions, a system of apprenticeship "by which the two races could gradually live themselves out of their old relations to each other."

At Gettysburg, Lincoln shifted gears and announced a new policy of liberation and social renewal. America, he said, was engaged in a great war testing whether it or any other nation "conceived in liberty and dedicated to the proposition that all men are created equal" could long endure. The war, he said, would decide whether "government of the people, by the people, for the people" would perish from the earth. But 20 days later when he unveiled his own postwar policy, it was obvious that *all* meant the same thing to Lincoln that it had always meant: all white people. In his Proclamation of Amnesty and Reconstruction, Lincoln said he would recognize any rebel state in which one-tenth of the white voters of 1860 took an oath of allegiance to the United States and organized a government which renounced slavery. What of black people? Slavery apart, Lincoln ignored them. Incredibly, the commander-in-chief of the U.S. Army abandoned his black soldiers to the passions of Confederate veterans who feared and hated them. Lincoln barely suggested "privately" that it would be a good thing for Southern states to extend the ballot "to the very intelligent [Negroes], and especially those who have fought gallantly in our ranks." But these were private sentiments, not public acts; and they were expressed in an extremely hesitant manner at that. Lincoln didn't require fair or equal treatment for the freedmen. In fact, he didn't make any demands at all. Reconstruction, Lincoln style, was going to be a Reconstruction of the white people by the white people and for the white people. . . .

Lincoln's assassination and the aggressive dissemination of the "Massa Linkun myth" pushed the real Lincoln with his real limitations into the background. And black people were soon pooling their pennies to erect a monument to the mythical emancipator. When, on April 14, 1876, this monument was unveiled, with President U.S. Grant and other high officials in attendance, Frederick Douglass punctured the myths and looked frankly at the man. Douglass praised Lincoln's growth, his rhetoric and his war services, but he also rehearsed his limitations and frailties.

Truth [Douglass said] *is proper and beautiful at all times and in all places, and it is never more proper and beautiful in any case than when speaking of a great public man whose example is likely to be commended for honor and imitation long after his departure to the solemn shades, the silent continent of eternity. It must be admitted, truth compels me to admit, even here in the presence of the monument we have erected to his memory, Abraham Lincoln was not, in the fullest sense of the word, either our man or our model. In his interests, in his associations, in his habits of thought, and in his prejudices, he was a white man. He was preeminently the white man's President, entirely devoted to the welfare of white men. He was ready and willing at any time during the first years of his administration to deny, postpone, and sacrifice the rights of humanity in the colored people to promote the welfare of the white people of this country. In all his education and feeling he was an American of the Americans.*

19   *Harry V. Jaffa*
Lincoln, the Emancipator

In Lincoln Park, Washington, D.C., is a monument that is perhaps not less notable than the great Lincoln Memorial itself. At its center is a statue of the standing figure of the Emancipator. His right hand, holding the Proclamation, rests upon a column displaying a bust in relief of George Washington. Lincoln's left arm and hand are extended, the index finger raised significantly. Beneath the extended arm is the crouched figure of a young Negro, the chain that joined the shackles upon his wrists broken. The face of the kneeling figure is almost expressionless; or perhaps one should say that the expression is that of one who is oblivious of everything present, whose vision is fixed upon a horizon that lies in the future. This scene embodies what most of us have been familiar with since childhood as the story-book version of how freedom came to the Negro slave in America. . . .

The tale told by the Freedman's Monument has, however, through the years achieved a standing not unlike other elements of popular mythology: for instance, that of George Washington and the cherry tree. It is said to be edifying, but hardly true. I cannot think of a better summary of recent historiography in regard to the actual episode than the following paragraph from

SOURCE. Harry V. Jaffa, "The Emancipation Proclamation," in Robert A. Goldwin, ed., *100 Years of Emancipation* (copyright © by the Public Affairs Conference Center, Kenyon College, 1963, 1964), pp. 1–23 *passim*. Reprinted by permission of the publisher and the author.

Professor Richard Hofstadter's essay on Lincoln in *The American Political Tradition:*

"The Emancipation Proclamation of January 1, 1863, had all the moral grandeur of a bill of lading. It contained no indictment of slavery, but simply based emancipation upon 'military necessity.' It expressly omitted the loyal slave states from its terms. Finally, it did not in fact free any slaves. For it excluded by detailed enumeration from the sphere covered in the Proclamation all the counties in Virginia and parishes in Louisiana that were occupied by Union troops and into which the government actually had the power to bring freedom. It simply declared free all slaves in 'the States and parts of States' where the people were in rebellion—that is to say, precisely where its effect could not reach. Beyond its propaganda value the Proclamation added nothing to what Congress had already done in the Confiscation Act."

Which view of the Emancipation Proclamation is the true one: that expressed in the memorial to the Great Emancipator by the grateful people who believed he had set them free, or that expressed in the sardonic accents of today's historical "revisionists"? I believe the only safe starting point is the recognition that the Emancipation Proclamation, like the policy of which it is the symbol if not the embodiment, is a thing of paradox. This much is recognized, to a degree, by Professor Hofstadter, who concludes, as do most historians, that "for all its limitations, the Emancipation Proclamation probably made genuine emancipation inevitable." It is sometimes even recognized that without its so-called limitations the Proclamation might not have been so efficacious to this end. This, however, does not decide the important question of whether or not "genuine emancipation" was its intended effect. There is even a school of thought that maintains that the real purpose of the Proclamation was to forestall, possibly even prevent, "genuine emancipation." It holds that Lincoln issued a Proclamation that literally freed no one, while diverting attention from his nonenforcement of the Confiscation Act of July 17, 1862, which the radicals in Congress, who were sincere emancipationists, had foisted upon him. We must accordingly ask, was the emancipating effect of the Proclamation the result of Lincoln's statecraft, was it in spite of that statecraft, or was it the outcome of events which had controlled him, and over which he had no really independent influence at all? . . .

The two Proclamations, of September 22, 1862, and January 1, 1863, are generally regarded as marking a sharp change in Lincoln's policy, from a "conservative" to a "liberal" policy, and, indeed, as changing the character of the war. . . .

To understand Lincoln's "conservatism" in the first great phase of the war, it is necessary to realize that everything he had fought for politically, from 1854 on, was now assured *if*, but only *if*, the Union was preserved. . . .

Both in the pre-inaugural period, and in the opening stages of the conflict, the danger of disunion, now the paramount danger, did not come from the forces of slavery alone. It came as well from the abolitionists. Now the name "abolitionist" was applied to a number of shades of opinion, although it is usually identified with the most extreme among them. However, there was a spectrum of opinions, beginning with those who insisted upon instant emancipation of all slaves, by any means, without regard to existing legality, without regard to the disruption and injury it would cause among both whites and blacks, and without indemnity or compensation of any kind. . . . As the spectrum proceeded from left to right, at some point the name "abolitionist" ceased to apply, and that of free-soiler replaced it. Lincoln was always a free-soiler, never an abolitionist, and in some respects Lincoln agreed with his Southern brethren that the abolitionists were a curse and an affliction. . . .

In the spectrum of antislavery opinions. . . Lincoln himself would have to be placed at the farthest limit of the extreme right. He was the most conservative of antislavery men. He did not, in any campaign, urge any form of emancipation other than that implied in the exclusion of slavery from the territories. First privately, later publicly, he favored gradual emancipation, and in the plan he recommended to Congress in December, 1862, the state action which he envisaged might have been extended over thirty-five years, until 1900. In the plan he put forward

while a Congressman, in 1848, for emancipation in the District of
Columbia, three factors were crucial: it had to be gradual,
voluntary (it had to be approved by a referendum in the District), and compensated. But Lincoln's task, as war came, was
to preserve the Union. All the emancipation Lincoln desired,
and probably a good deal more, was assured *if* the Union en-
dured. If it did not endure, all the lets and hindrances exerted
upon slavery by the free states in the Union would be removed.
The extreme abolitionists, in the supposed purity of their principles, would have abandoned the four million slaves to their
fate. As the secession crisis developed, however, the attitude of
the border states trembled in the balance. Virginia did not cast
its lot with the Confederacy until after Sumter, and when it did
so the western counties broke away, eventually to form a new
state, a case of secession from secession. Tennessee went with
the South, although Unionist sentiment was strong; many a Ten-
nesseean marched with the Federal armies, and many a family
was divided. But Missouri and Kentucky were slave states which,
with Maryland and Delaware, remained faithful to the Union
cause, as they might not have done had a man they trusted less,
whom they regarded as less one of their own, occupied the
presidential chair. The strategic importance of Kentucky and
Missouri can be seen by a glance at the map. Lincoln himself
thought that the military task of conquering the South would not
have been possible without them. "Neutrality" by Kentucky
would have denied the Union armies vital communications. If
we think then of the range of Unionist opinion, and not merely
of antislavery opinion, we will begin to appreciate the political
task Lincoln faced. Border-state Unionists, supported by large
and powerful elements of conservative Democrats and old-line
Whigs throughout the free states, would fight for the Union but
not against slavery. Abolitionists, on the other hand, would not
fight for the Union, but would fight against slavery. When we
realize that these extremes were about as willing to fight each
other as to fight secession, we realize that preserving the Union
meant, for Lincoln, first of all, creating an effective political
coalition. Fighting the war was always secondary to keeping
alive the political coalition willing to fight the war. . . .

. . . In a message to Congress of March 6, 1862, Lincoln recommended the adoption of a joint resolution in these words:

"Resolved, That the United States, in order to cooperate with any State which may adopt gradual abolition of slavery, give to such State pecuniary aid, to be used by such State, in its discretion, to compensate it for the inconvenience, public and private, produced by such change of system."

Lincoln explained to the Congress, which adopted his proposed resolution a month later (April 10), that if the border slave-states would make *any* beginning toward emancipation, it would strike an almost mortal blow at the hopes of the rebellion, which believed that if they could force any kind of recognition of any part of their Confederacy, they would eventually be joined by the loyal slave-states. Lincoln realized this resolution had no practical effect in itself; it was "merely initiatory." But it is also exemplary of Lincoln's cautious, step-by-step way of moving to change the basis of policy from plain, unqualified Unionism, to a Unionism that recognized the necessity of anti-slavery dynamism. Two months later, on May 9, Lincoln issued his famous proclamation countermanding the emancipation order of General David Hunter, who had declared that as Georgia, Florida, and South Carolina were under martial law, and as martial law and slavery were incompatible, that the slaves in these states were free. Lincoln said that "neither General Hunter, nor any other person has been authorized . . . to make proclamation declaring the slaves of any state free . . . [and] whether it be competent for me, as Commander-in-Chief . . . to declare the slaves of any State or States free; and whether at any time, or in any case, it shall become a necessity indispensable to the maintenance of the government to examine such power, are questions which I reserve to myself. . . . " Here, written upon the wall, for all to see who would see, was the shadow of the Emancipation Proclamation. But Lincoln did not stop here. In this masterful document, while with one hand he revoked a proclamation that was loudly acclaimed by the radicals, . . . with the other he moved to prepare the public for a policy of emancipation that would mean infinitely more,

when it came, than any which might have proceeded from
overly-enthusiastic radical generals. He reminded the nation of
the joint resolution which Congress had recently passed upon
his recommendation. Then he addressed to the border-state
men these words:

"The resolution . . . was adopted by large majorities in both
branches of Congress, and now stands an authentic, definite,
and solemn proposal of the Nation to the States and people
most interested. . . . To the people of these States now, I
mostly appeal. I do not argue—I beseech you to make the
arguments for yourselves. You cannot, if you would, be blind
to the signs of the times.

"This proposal makes common cause for a common object,
casting no reproaches upon any. It acts not the Pharisee. The
change it contemplates would come gently as the dews of
Heaven, not rending or wrecking anything. Will you not embrace it? So much good has not been done by one effort in all
past time, as on the Providence of God, it is now your high
privilege to do. May the vast future not have to lament that
you have neglected it."

Alas, the vast future has much cause to lament. The majority
of the border-state men, loyal Unionists though they were, would
not accept the implicit condemnation of slavery which in their
hearts they felt would be implied even if they themselves took
a single step to abolish slavery upon their soil. Though Lincoln, with words of beauty, turned away every possible reproach
such as they had been accustomed to hear from abolitionists,
there was a mark of *hubris* upon them, as upon all men touched
by slavery in that period, as indeed it was upon the radical
abolitionists. Lincoln was to address the border-state delega-
tions in Congress in July, before they left for home, and in
majestic and pathetic language, rang every change upon the
foregoing theme. But to no avail. In their reply to him they
said:

"Confine yourself to your constitutional authority; confine
your subordinates within the same limits; conduct this war solely

for the purpose of restoring the Constitution to its legitimate authority; concede to each State and its loyal citizens their just rights, and we are wedded to you by indissoluble ties."

Lincoln had told the border-state Congressmen that, if the war continued, "the institution in your states will be extinguished by mere friction and abrasion. . . . It will be gone, and you will have nothing valuable in lieu of it. . . . How much better . . . to take the step which, at once shortens the war, and secures substantial compensation for that which is sure to be wholly lost in any other event." By friction and abrasion, Lincoln meant that, as Federal armies moved forward upon the soil of slave states, rebel or loyal, the problems of dealing with the Negroes became ever larger and ever more complicated. Obviously, the fugitive-slave law, which Lincoln had so carefully pledged himself to enforce in his Inaugural Address, could not be enforced in the midst of war. For example, the task of distinguishing the fugitives of loyal masters from the fugitives of rebels, was administratively insuperable. But as the war placed greater and greater strains upon the human and material resources of the sections, there loomed ever larger the fact that the slave population of the deep South nearly equalled that of the whites, and was little less than half of the white population in the upper South. One reason why the Confederacy could put so high a proportion of its white male population under arms was that Negro labor did the drudging tasks which every society requires, and which must be done by one set of hands if not by another. Slavery was what the rebel states were fighting for, and slavery enabled them to fight for slavery. Lincoln's cautious, constitutional conservatism was the necessary stabilizing factor while he bound up the loose ties of Unionism, as he organized the Union to fight for its life. But once the fight was organized, and became increasingly desperate, once abolitionists and border-state Unionists, neither of whom would fight for the other, had been committed to the same cause by their blood in battle, the policy had to change. The task was no longer to make them pull in harness together, but to strike blows that would kill the rebellion. And of all these blows, none held such power as that directed against slavery by the two proclamations.

Although the two proclamations were, as Lincoln insistently described them, war measures, measures of military necessity, and justified under the Constitution only as such, Lincoln's political (as distinct from military) emancipation policy, continued to occupy his thoughts; indeed, nothing occupied him more. There is no place here to consider the many measures that Congress had passed before the proclamations. Most important was the second Confiscation Act, of July 17, 1862. This was, as J. G. Randall says, primarily a treason and confiscation act. It enacted that all slaves of persons hereafter engaged in rebellion, or the slaves of persons who in any way gave aid and comfort to rebellion, and all slaves captured or deserted from such persons, should be forever free. Although Lincoln signed this act, he undoubtedly considered it neither constitutional nor wise. But he was having enough trouble with the radicals without vetoing a law which could not have any greater effect than he wished it to have. In any case, Lincoln always held to the conviction, finally expressed with surpassing majesty in the Gettysburg Address and the Second Inaugural, that slavery was the sin of the whole nation, not of a section. If for the remission of that sin, the Lord in His infinite justice might exact a price in blood from the whole nation, was it less the duty of a wise statesmanship ultimately to share the money cost among the whole nation? Lincoln's Emancipation Proclamations, unlike the Congressional measures, were not a punishment for anything; they were rather a summons to the slaves, not to rise against their masters, but to shift the power of their labor from the oppressors to their liberators. And so they presently did. But for the nonmilitary settlement of the slavery question, Lincoln pressed on with his plan for voluntary, compensated emancipation.

Space does not permit a full consideration of the plan that Lincoln presented to Congress in his annual message of December 1, 1862, a message which came after approximately two-thirds of the one hundred days had passed, in which the rebellion had warning of the impending final proclamation of emancipation. Lincoln recommended that his plan be embodied in articles amendatory of the Constitution, so that no question could arise as to its constitutionality. The first feature of the plan was the offer of United States bonds, in an amount that would be a multiple of the number of slaves in each emancipating state, and a fair average evaluation for each slave. What this would be, Lincoln did not attempt to determine in the message. Next, the adoption of emancipation schemes by each state would be a matter of state action. There was no federal coercion contemplated; it was a pure "grant-in-aid" scheme, such as Congress now enacts in every session, and any state could leave it as well as take it, as far as the law was concerned. Finally, emancipation was to be gradual, and might extend until the year 1900. Lincoln then proposed, in a distinct article, that Congress provide compensation for loyal masters whose slaves had either escaped, or otherwise gained their freedom by the chances of war. Finally, in still another article, he sought definite authorization for Congress to appropriate money for the colonization abroad of the freed slaves. As we review Lincoln's plan we must be struck by the almost Jeffersonian fundamentalism wherewith he sought constitutional authority for policies which carried the federal government into a wholly new sphere of legislation; and how, while exercising the leadership of the President of the whole United States, for a national plan, he tried to secure the sanction of the people in the states, acting through state authority, to carry it into effect. Even as, years before, in proposing compensated emancipation for the District of Columbia, he had made the proposal dependent upon a vote of the citizens of the District, he here proposed that an amendment to the Constitution be passed, not to emancipate the slaves, but to authorize the federal government to pay the states, *if they wished* to emancipate the slaves. But behind this Lincolnian "voluntarism" lay the fact . . . : no matter what action the states did or did not take, slavery was doomed. Lincoln's plan, which never passed from Congress to the states, remains as a model of that charity which he preached and practiced but which, like the counsels of perfection, was beyond the capacities of the men for whose sake he devised it.

Let us then . . . ask again the questions with which we began. In my opinion, the Freedman's Monument is a true depiction, not of an isolated event of the war, but of Lincoln's whole policy. Lincoln *is* the Great Emancipator, not because of what he did on January 1, 1863, but because of everything he did, and said, from his first speech against the Kansas-Nebraska Act, until his Second Inaugural, and indeed until the last day of his life. In a sense, it is true that Lincoln never intended to emancipate the Negro: what he intended was to emancipate the American republic from the curse of slavery, a curse which lay upon both races, and which in different ways enslaved them both. This might have happened "gently as the dews of Heaven, not rending or wrecking anything," if the slave power had accepted his election, and settled slowly and seriously to deal with the gradual and peaceable "ultimate extinction" implied in the containment of slavery. It might have still come with much gentleness, if the border states had started the process of voluntary emancipation, which would have broken the hopes of the Confederacy. It came instead with the hard and pitiless hand of war. Lincoln's message was always peace, but like other messengers of peace, he brought not peace but a sword. In the last analysis, it is absurd to characterize Lincoln's policy as either "liberal" or "conservative," if by these terms we imply a mere party or sectarian position. His policy encompassed everything that was viable in every element of opinion, by which, of course, we exclude the proslavery and antislavery extremists, because there was nothing viable in what they proposed. As the proslavery extremists utterly disregarded the humanity of the Negro, so did the abolitionists disregard utterly the element of consent required for the just acts of government. In fact, the two were more akin than opposed, even in principle, for what both disregarded was at bottom the same thing—the principle of equality.

20   *J. G. Randall and Richard N. Current*
Race Relations in the White House

It would be an oversimplification to say that the Thirteenth Amendment made freemen out of slaves, or even that it was intended to do so. The amendment grew out of a variety of motives, as Henry Wilson said. Some who favored it were motivated by a sense of "religious obligation" or by "humane considerations," but others by "feelings of resentment" against slaveholders, whom they blamed for starting the war. The largest number were moved by "prudential considerations merely," Wilson believed (and, though Wilson did not say so, Lincoln himself was moved by such considerations mainly). "They accepted emancipation not so much from any heartfelt conversion to the doctrine of anti-slavery as from the conviction that the removal of slavery had become a military, if not a political, necessity." The "foul spirit of caste" still "lurked within the hearts of many" who applauded the progress of emancipation. So long as the former slaves suffered from the prejudice of the white community, they would not be free *men* but only free *Negroes.*

The Negroes freed during the war, like those already free when the war began, had to make their way against serious handicaps, whether as soldiers or as civilians and whether as residents of the North or of the South. The plight of the new freedmen was sometimes desperate. Before the end of 1863 fifty thousand of them, mostly women and children, were adrift in the lower Mississippi Valley, with little shelter and practically no food, except occasional army rations of crackers and dried beef. "At present, hundreds of the blacks would gladly return

SOURCE. Reprinted by permission of Dodd, Mead & Company, Inc. from *Lincoln the President,* Volume IV, *Last Full Measure* by J. G. Randall and Richard N. Current, pp. 315–321. Copyright 1955 by Dodd, Mead & Company, Inc.

to slavery, to avoid the hardships of freedom," Lincoln was informed. Even the most fortunate of the freedmen faced hardships and dangers to which white men were immune. Negro soldiers ran an added risk (if captured, they could not count upon the usual protection of the laws of war) and Negro laborers in the army were paid, at first, according to their color and not according to their work. Even Negroes born free and living in the so-called free states lacked many of the privileges ordinarily associated with freedom. They could not enter certain occupations, they could not always travel without restriction, and they could not vote or hold office in most of the states, including Illinois.

Before the end of the war the free Negroes and their white friends began a campaign in the state legislatures and in Congress to free the colored population from discriminatory laws. Most of the anti-Negro legislation of Illinois (but not the restriction of suffrage to the whites) was repealed early in 1865. At about the same time Congress passed and the President signed a bill setting up the Freedmen's Bureau to care for refugees. Senator Sumner, who had got Negroes admitted to practice in the Federal courts, tried to obtain for them the privilege of riding on the Washington street cars. Representative Stevens began to talk of confiscating Southern estates and dividing them among the freedmen—"forty acres and a mule" to each family head. The Fourteenth Amendment, presumably designed to protect Negroes in their civil rights, and the Fifteenth Amendment, to guarantee their right to vote, were to be adopted in the early post-war years. These were only the beginning steps in an undertaking which, nearly a century later, was still to fall short of complete success.

The Negro's advancement was hindered less by laws or the absence of laws than by popular attitudes—the "foul spirit of caste," as Henry Wilson called it. Lincoln himself had yielded to this spirit when, in 1862, he urged the resettlement of freed Negroes in foreign lands, with the argument that the white and black races could not be expected to live together in harmony within the United States. While some Negro leaders approved the idea of colonizing their people outside the country, others denounced it, and one wrote impertinently to the President: "Pray tell us is our right to a home in this country less than your own?" Lincoln not only abandoned the colonization idea but also proceeded to give repeated demonstrations that, whether or not Negroes and whites could mingle harmoniously in the country at large, they could certainly do so within his own official home.

He opened the White House to colored visitors as no President had done before, and he received them in a spirit which no President has matched since. At his New Year's Day reception in 1864 "four colored men, of genteel exterior and with the manners of gentlemen, joined in the throng that crowded the Executive Mansion, and were presented to the President of the United States," as the Washington *Morning Chronicle* reported the unprecedented news. There was no scene. "We are neither amalgamationists nor advocates of the leveling of all social distinctions," the *Chronicle* commented; "but we rejoice that we have a President who is a democrat by fact as well as by nature." On the Fourth of July that same year Lincoln gave permission to the colored schools of the District of Columbia to hold a celebration on the White House grounds, and on August 6 he allowed Negroes to assemble on the grounds in day-long ceremonies observing the national day of humiliation and prayer which he had ordained. In these and other ways he set an example of tolerance for all his fellow countrymen.

Lincoln invited and welcomed prominent individual Negroes. Frederick Douglass met him several times at the Soldiers' Home and paid at least three calls at the White House. He made his last visit as a guest at the reception on the night of the second inauguration. As he approached the door that night he was seized by two policemen and forbidden to enter, but managed to bolt past them. On the inside two other policemen took hold of him. He thought they were going to lead him to the President; instead, they led him out through a window on a plank. At the door again, he appealed to a guest going in to tell Lincoln he was there. In a moment he was invited into the East Room. There, in the presence of an elegant company of ladies and gentlemen, Lincoln said in a voice heard all around: "Here comes my friend

Douglass." He shook hands cordially with him and immediately engaged him in conversation. Afterwards Douglass recalled:

"In all my interviews with Mr. Lincoln I was impressed with his entire freedom from popular prejudice against the colored race. He was the first great man that I talked with in the United States freely, who in no single instance reminded me of the difference between himself and myself, of the difference of color, and I thought that all the more remarkable because he came from a state where there were black laws."

Another former slave, the remarkable Sojourner Truth, had a friendly and unstrained conversation with Lincoln when she dropped in to see him, October 20, 1864. He obliged her by signing his name in her autograph book, for "Aunty Sojourner Truth," as he wrote. When a delegation of Negro Baptist clergymen sought an appointment with him, he had them shown in and nodded his head in assent as they requested permission to preach to colored soldiers. He gave hearty encouragement to another Negro preacher who wished to send missionaries among the escaping slaves, the "contrabands." Numbers of other colored people also came to him, and all went away gratified at their cordial and respectful treatment.

He did more than send his Negro supplicants away with kind words. When a thousand New Orleans Negroes sent a two-man delegation to Washington (in January, 1864) he responded by assigning James A. McKaye, of the American Freedmen's Inquiry Commission, to look into their needs and wants. McKayé went to New Orleans, attended a colored mass meeting, and learned that they desired public schools, recognition as human beings, and the abolition of the black codes. Lincoln, apparently impressed by the behavior of the Louisiana Negroes, was willing to grant them a little more than they demanded. In March he sent a private letter to Michael Hahn, congratulating him on his inauguration as the first free-State governor of Louisiana, and adding: "Now you are about to have a convention, which, among other things, will probably define the elective franchise. I barely suggest to your private consideration, whether some of the colored people may not be let in—as, for instance, the very intelligent, and especially those who fought gallantly in our ranks.

They would probably help, in some trying time to come, to keep the jewel of liberty within the family of freedom."

In the presence of his Negro visitors Lincoln was careful not to use expressions or tell stories which might offend them. In the presence of white men approaching him in the Negro's behalf he was not always so careful, but he was equally responsive to their appeals. "Sometime during the year 1864," according to a memoir left by Henry Samuels, several representatives of the Committee for Recruiting Colored Troops were ushered into the President's private room by Secretary Stanton. "The President was seated at his desk with his long legs on the top of it, his hands on his head and looking exactly like a huge katydid or grass-hopper." He quietly listened until his petitioners had finished, then "turned his head and jocularly said, with one of those peculiar smiles of his": "Well, gentlemen, you wish the pay of 'Cuffie' raised." The youthfully brash and earnest Samuels objected: "Excuse me, Mr. Lincoln, the term 'Cuffie' is not in our vernacular. What we want is that the wages of the American Colored Laborer be equalized with those of the American White Laborer." Lincoln replied: "I stand corrected, young man, but you know I am by birth a Southerner and in our section that term is applied without any idea of an offensive nature. I will, however, at the earliest possible moment do all in my power to accede to your request." About a month later the war department issued an order requiring that Negro teamsters and other laborers employed by the army be paid at the same rate as white men doing the same kinds of work.

Though relatively few Negroes ever saw Lincoln, and still fewer talked with him, Negroes everywhere came to think of him as their friend. They were not backward in expressing their regard for him. The colored people of Baltimore, to show their appreciation of the "distinguished services of President Lincoln in the cause of human freedom," contributed $580.75 to have a copy of the Bible bound in purple velvet, mounted in gold, engraved with a representation of Lincoln striking the shackles from a slave, and enclosed in a walnut case lined with white silk. This imposing volume they presented to the President at the White House in September, 1864. "I can only say now, as I have often said before, it has always been a sentiment with me that all mankind should be free," Lincoln remarked, in thanking the colored delegation. "In regard to the great book, I can only say it is the best gift which God has ever given man." The action of the Baltimore colored people, he told Frank B. Carpenter, gave him more real satisfaction than any other public testimonial he ever received. . . .

Lincoln, dead, was nearly deified by many Negroes. "There were no truer mourners, when all were sad, than the poor colored people who crowded the streets, joined the procession, and exhibited their woe, bewailing the loss of him whom they regarded as a benefactor and father." So wrote Secretary Welles, after the funeral ceremonies in Washington. And many years later a Negro historian wrote: "The deep, nation-wide grief of the Negroes was an outward sign that their generation would hold the name of the martyred President in everlasting remembrance. The colored people beheld in Lincoln a father image; he was 'the chieftest of ten thousand, and altogether lovely.' His death burdened every black with a personal sense of loss. . . ."

PART FIVE

Lincoln and the Union

Lincoln and the Union

And this issue embraces more than the fate of these United States. . . . It forces us to ask: Is there, in all republics, this inherent and fatal weakness? Must a government, of necessity, be too *strong* for the liberties of its own people, or too *weak* to maintain its own existence?

LINCOLN, MESSAGE TO CONGRESS, JULY 4, 1861

Was it possible to lose the nation, and yet preserve the constitution? By general law life *and* limb must be protected; yet often a limb must be amputated to save a life; but a life is never wisely given to save a limb. I felt that measures, otherwise unconstitutional, might become lawful, by becoming indispensable to the preservation of the constitution, through the preservation of the nation.

LINCOLN TO A. G. HODGES, APRIL 4, 1864

The Union with him in sentiment rose to the sublimity of a religious mysticism; while his ideas of its structure and formation in logic rested upon nothing but the subtleties of a sophism!

ALEXANDER H. STEPHENS, 1870

The only thing like passion or infatuation in the man was the passion for the Union of These States.

WALT WHITMAN, 1886

Beyond his own country some of us recall his name as the greatest among those associated with the cause of popular

159

government. . . . His own intense experience of the weakness of democracy did not sour him, nor would any similar
experience of later times have been likely to do so.

LORD CHARNWOOD, 1916

Lincoln loved the Union as the great symbol of human
unity. He identified himself with it in the sense that he
attributed its greatness and his own private fortunes to the
principles of free society.

HENRY ALONZO MYERS, 1945

Lincoln reached manhood and entered politics in the 1830's,
when the surviving fathers of the Republic, like Charles Carroll
and James Madison, were disappearing from the scene. For
his generation, the Revolution and the Constitutional Convention
were still near enough in time to be a vivid memory, yet sufficiently remote to have become a heroic legend. During the
1840's, the pride of a young nation overflowed in an effusion
of the spirit of "manifest destiny." But Lincoln, never an ardent
expansionist, belonged to that school of patriots who found
America's special destiny in the opportunity to test and demonstrate the viability of self-government. His ultimate commitment
was not to the Union itself but to the experiment in democracy
that it represented. From a nation that made a mockery of the
Declaration of Independence, he wrote in 1855, he would prefer
to emigrate—even to Russia, "where despotism can be taken
pure, without the base alloy of hypocrisy." The legal foundation
of the Union was the Constitution, which Lincoln as president
had sworn to "preserve, protect, and defend." Yet in the desperate struggle to save the Union, he was driven to actions of
doubtful constitutionality that drew charges of tyranny from his
political enemies. J.G. Randall, in the following excerpts from
one of his earliest books, discusses Lincoln's use of arbitrary
power and the extent to which he resembled a dictator. According to William B. Hesseltine, the triumph of nationalism
achieved by Lincoln overturned the old federal republic and

marked the "death of states' rights." Nathaniel W. Stephenson, the first professional historian to write a biography of Lincoln, sees him as the "colossal central figure" in the achievement of a sense of nationality that was still incomplete, even among Northerners, in 1861. James A. Rawley, author of several books on the Civil War era, likewise finds evidence in Lincoln's writings of a new and less legalistic definition of the nation. The final selection in this chapter is taken from the brief but perceptive study of Lincoln by Sir Kenneth Wheare, Rector of Exeter College, Oxford, and an authority on comparative government. Wheare probes the meaning of Lincoln's nationalism by examining the reasons why he could not acquiesce in peaceable secession.

21   *J. G. Randall*
The Constitution Stretched but Not Subverted

It is indeed a striking fact that Lincoln, who stands forth in popular conception as a great democrat, the exponent of liberty and of government by the people, was driven by circumstances to the use of more arbitrary power than perhaps any other President has seized. Probably no President has carried the power of proclamation and executive order (independently of Congress) so far as did Lincoln. It would not be easy to state what Lincoln conceived to be the limit of his powers. He carried his executive authority to the extent of freeing the slaves by proclamation, setting up a whole scheme of state-making for the purpose of reconstruction, suspending the *habeas corpus* privilege, proclaiming martial law, enlarging the army and navy beond the limits fixed by existing law, and spending public money without congressional appropriation. Some of his important

SOURCE. J. G. Randall, *Constitutional Problems under Lincoln,* Revised Edition (Urbana, Illinois: The University of Illinois Press, 1951), pp. 513–515, 519–522. Reprinted by permission of the publisher.

measures were taken under the consciousness that they belonged within the domain of Congress. The national legislature was merely permitted to ratify these measures, or else to adopt the futile alternative of refusing consent to an accomplished fact. We have seen how the first national use of conscription, in connection with the Militia Act of 1862, was an instance of presidential legislation. We have also noted the exercise of judicial functions by Lincoln or those acting under his authority, in regions under martial law, in Southern territory under Union occupation, in the application of military justice, in the performance of quasi-judicial functions by executive departments, and in the creation of "special war courts" such as the "provisional court of Louisiana." It thus appears that the President, while greatly enlarging his executive powers, seized also legislative and judicial functions as well.

Lincoln's view of the war power is significant. He believed that rights of war were vested in the President, and that as President he had extraordinary legal resources which Congress lacked. For example, he promulgated the "laws of war" to regulate the conduct of the armies; and in vetoing the Wade-Davis bill of 1864 he questioned the constitutional competency of Congess to abolish slavery in the States at a time when his own edict of emancipation had been in force for eighteen months. Lincoln tended to the view that in war the Constitution restrains Congress more than it restrains the President. Yet the view of the Supreme Court was that Congress may exercise belligerent powers and that in the use of these powers over the enemy the restraints of the Constitution do not apply. Lincoln's view, under pressure of severe circumstance, led naturally to that course which has been referred to as his "dictatorship"; and, as illustrated in the *Prize Cases,* it produced uncertainty as to the legality of the war. Though the validity of Lincoln's acts was sustained by a majority of the court—which could hardly have decided otherwise on so vital a political question— yet four dissenting judges held that the President's action alone was not sufficient to institute a legal state of war. Lincoln's plea in defense, to the effect that his acts within the legislative domain could be legalized by congressional ratification, could hardly be accepted as consistent with the constitutional separation of powers; and this whole phase of the President's conduct illustrates not so much a permanently acceptable principle, but rather Lincoln's ability to retain popular confidence while doing irregular things. It should be added that Lincoln excelled in human reasonableness, and that his character included not only a readiness to act in an emergency, but also a high regard for the rule of law. . . .

His humane sympathy, his humor, his lawyerlike caution, his common sense, his fairness toward opponents, his dislike of arbitrary rule, his willingness to take the people into his confidence and to set forth patiently the reasons for unusual measures—all these elements of his character operated to modify and soften the acts of overzealous subordinates and to lessen the effect of harsh measures upon individuals. He was criticized for leniency as often as for severity. Though there were arbitrary arrests under Lincoln, there was no thoroughgoing arbitrary government. The Government smarted under great abuse without passing either an Espionage Act or a Sedition Law. Freedom of speech was preserved to the point of permitting the most disloyal utterances. While a book could be written on the suppression of certain newspapers, the military control of the telegraph, the seizure of particular editions, the withholding of papers from the mails, and the arrest of editors, yet in a broad view of the whole situation such measures appear so far from typical that they sink into comparative insignificance. There was no real censorship, and in the broad sense the press was unhampered though engaging in activities distinctly harmful to the Government. As to Lincoln's attitude in this matter, it should be remembered that in general he advised non-interference with the press, and that he applied this policy prominently in the case of the Chicago *Times*.

To suppose that Lincoln's suspension of the *habeas corpus* privilege set aside all law would be erroneous. The suspension was indeed a serious matter; but men were simply arrested on suspicion, detained for a while, and then released. The whole effect of their treatment was milder than if they had been punished through the ordinary processes of justice. As to the military trial of civilians, it should be noticed that the typical use of the military commission was legitimate; for these commissions were commonly used to try citizens in military areas for military crimes. Where citizens in proximity to the Union army were engaged in sniping or bushwhacking, in bridge burning or the destruction of railroad or telegraph lines, they were tried, as they should have been, by military commission; and this has occasioned little comment, though there were hundreds of cases. The prominence of the cases of Vallandigham and Milligan should not obscure the larger fact that these cases were exceptional: in other words, the military trial of citizens for non-military offenses in peaceful areas was far from typical. It was thus a rare use of the military commission that was declared illegal in the Milligan case.

Legally, the Civil War stands out as an eccentric period, a time when constitutional restraints did not fully operate and when the "rule of law" largely broke down. It was a period when opposite and conflicting situations coexisted, when specious arguments and legal fictions were put forth to excuse extraordinary measures. It was a period during which the line was blurred between executive, legislative, and judicial functions; between State and Federal powers; and between military and civil procedures. International law as well as constitutional interpretation was stretched. The powers grasped by Lincoln caused him to be denounced as a "dictator." Yet civil liberties were not annihilated and no thoroughgoing dictatorship was established. There was nothing like a Napoleonic *coup d'état*. No undue advantage was taken of the emergency to force arbitrary rule upon the country or to promote personal ends. A comparison with European examples shows that Lincoln's government lacked many of the earmarks of dictatorial rule. His administration did not, as in some dictatorships, employ criminal violence to destroy its opponents and perpetuate its power. It is significant that Lincoln half expected to be defeated in 1864. The people were free to defeat him, if they chose, at the polls. The Constitution, while stretched, was not subverted. The measures taken were recognized by the people as exceptional; and they were no more exceptional than the emergency for which they were used. Looking beyond the period called "reconstruction," the net effect, as Lincoln had said, was not to give the nation a taste for extreme rule any more than a patient, because of the use of emetics during illness, acquires a taste for them in normal life. In a legal study of the war the two most significant facts are perhaps these: the wide extent of the war powers; and, in contrast to that, the manner in which the men in authority were nevertheless controlled by the American people's sense of constitutional government.

22 *William B. Hesseltine*
The Death of States' Rights

The election of 1864 demonstrated, conclusively and finally, that Abraham Lincoln had made a nation. At the same moment on the battlefields of the Civil War the constitutional riddle of the American federal system was being resolved. Within a few months of the election Grant and Lee met at Appomattox Courthouse, and the Southern Confederacy—which had been founded upon the dogmas of states' rights—collapsed. But in the North, Abraham Lincoln had already determined that the nation was supreme and states' rights outmoded in theory and practice.

Under Lincoln's leadership the national government had won military control over the manpower of the states. A national economic system based on new national banks, the nation-made financial centers, government-subsidized railroads, and a protective tariff had grown strong during the war. And, of necessity, state politics revolved in the national orbit.

In 1860 the nation had been on the eve of dissolution. National institutions that had long existed had fallen apart. The

SOURCE. Condensed from *Lincoln and the War Governors*, by William B. Hesseltine, pp. 385–392. Copyright 1948 by Alfred A. Knopf, Inc. Reprinted by permission of the publisher.

Methodist and Baptist churches had divided, the Whig Party had disintegrated, and the Democratic Party had split. In that year the Republican Party, which Abraham Lincoln was to make into a new nationalizing agency, had only a nominal existence. It was, in truth, only a series of state parties, lacking either unity or a coherent program. Its orientation was in the states, and state politicians led it.

In 1860 the Republican platform had solemnly declared that "the Rights of the States . . . must and shall be preserved," and had added: "the maintenance inviolate of the rights of the States, and especially the right of each state to order and control its own domestic institutions according to its own judgment exclusively is essential to that balance of powers on which the perfection and endurance of our political fabric depends."

And in 1860 the Republicans had taken pains to "denounce the lawless invasion by armed forces of the soil of any State or Territory, no matter under what pretext, as among the gravest of crimes."

Within four years the exigencies of the Civil War had made a mockery of these platform phrases. . . . By suspending the writ of habeas corpus, by conscription, and by the use of troops at the polls, Lincoln had saved the Republican Party and had made it an instrument to save the Union.

But states' rights were dead. Their death was clear in January 1865 as the legislatures met and the governors, old and new, spoke again on the state of the Union. The contrast with 1861 was significant of the changes the war had wrought. In the January after Lincoln's first election the governors had given directions to the President-elect on the policies of his administration. . . . But by January 1865 experience had chastened the governors, and the torch of leadership had passed from their hands. . . .

. . . Lincoln had triumphed over the governors, and the nation had emerged victorious over the states. The triumph was, in truth, the product of many factors. Among them, and fortunately for his Union-saving purposes, was the situation that had nearly always enabled Lincoln to deal with the governors individually. Divided opinion between the conservatives and the radicals among them had made the President's moderating position easier. The governors, moreover, were not in the habit of consulting together, and their contacts with one another were comparatively few. . . .

In addition to the advantage of dealing with the governors separately, Lincoln had an enormously swollen patronage to dispense for national rather than state ends. The civilian personnel of the departments grew under the needs of the war, but no part of that patronage was at the disposal of the governors. The President and the cabinet officers consulted with congressmen on local appointments, but a governor's recommendation was worthless to an office-seeker. Moreover, the military patronage was at the President's disposal. Governors might appoint company and regimental officers, but promotions from grade to grade and the selection of general officers depended on the President. The army and the civil patronage—as the experiences in the border states, in Ohio in 1863, and in the campaign of 1864 proved—put the Republican Party exclusively in Lincoln's hands.

But in the long run Lincoln's victory over the governors was the triumph of a superior intellect. Of the sixty-three chief executives of the states with whom Lincoln dealt in the four years of the Civil War, only Horatio Seymour could approach the President in quality of mind. Seymour's partial success in blocking conscription was a tribute to his intellectual power. Had he possessed Lincoln's understanding of men and his political skill, Seymour might have prevented the destruction of states' rights. But Seymour stood alone. The other governors lacked the clear insight that Lincoln and Seymour displayed. . . . When they became neurotic, hysterical, "skeered," or when they became contentious, arrogant, and imperative, Abraham Lincoln remained calm, keeping his balance—and keeping his eye on the goal of saving the Union.

And this, above all, made Lincoln the architect of the new nation. The victory of nationalism over localism, of centralization over states' rights, was, in the last analysis, a victory of a keener intellect over men of lesser minds. The new nation that emerged from the Civil War was not solely the result of the military defeat of the armies of Robert E. Lee. It was equally the result of the political victory that Abraham Lincoln's mind and personality won over the governors of the Northern states.

23   *Nathaniel W. Stephenson*
Completing the Mold of Nationality

. . . We have got in the habit of saying that North and South had been developing upon different lines during 40 years before the war, but have we followed out all the ramifications of that idea? Have we given enough consideration to the fact— obvious, it seems to me—that while the North had passed into a second stage on the road to nationalization it was still far from the ultimate stage? Though the smaller territorial units had lost their hold upon men's imagination, though an economic community had been established, there was not yet established, when the first gun was fired in 1861, the power to effect a complete, uniform, national reaction. A wave of passion is not necessarily an expression of nationality. The fury that swept the North in 1861 deserves more analytical study than has sometimes been accorded it. That, at the back of it, something in the way of a national spirit had arrived is past the question. But it was still an unsolidified sense of nationality that was cut across and broken up by disintegrating tendencies—tendencies which were producing temperamental units, class units, highly dangerous to the whole; and there was still lacking that profound spiritual cohesion which transforms a horde into a nation. . . . The truth is, the political and economic molds in which northern life had been contained were broken up between 1830 and 1860, but the imaginative molds,

SOURCE. Nathaniel W. Stephenson, "Lincoln and the Progress of Nationality in the North," American Historical Association *Annual Report*, Vol. I (1919), pp. 357–362.

which are so much more intimate than the political ones, were not broken up. To reconstruct certain of these molds, to make possible a new fusion of their contents, to establish a new channel for political imagination, was the great task in the development of American nationality not yet complete in 1861.

In the accomplishment of that task the colossal central figure is, of course, Lincoln. Therefore, his views on his own role, on the function of his office, are so intensely interesting. What, then, was Lincoln's conception of that community, not fully realized in his own day, which he calls in his messages our National Union? How did he expect the people of this Union, weltering as they were in diversity, to arise out of their confusions one nation? As an expression of their nationalism, how did he conceive his own high office?

It is a great misfortune that Lincoln has not left us a general statement of his views on any of these points. What lay back of his actions, what in time he might have formulated, we must infer, as best we can, from certain crucial events and from a relatively small number of utterances. But a few things are plain: First, his conception of the permanent form of our National Union was a federal one. If there is any belief of his that can be proved beyond peradventure from his own words it is his acceptance of the group of States as the fixed term in our political science. Lincoln was not a Hamiltonian. He did not hesitate to declare "that the maintenance inviolate of the rights of the States and especially the right of each State to control its domestic institutions according to its own judgment exclusively, is essential to that balance of powers on which the perfection and endurance of our political fabric depend."

Secondly, Lincoln conceived our National Union as preeminently a people's government. This, in spite of our literary fondness for the last sentence of the Gettysburg address, is too often forgotten. Whether we like it or not, we must see Lincoln as a statesman of the masses. Thus he conceived himself. With startling explicitness—for when was Lincoln not explicit?—he committed himself to the belief that the mass, the laborers, were the part of the Nation entitled to the greatest share of its benefits. . . .

The third main feature of Lincoln's conception of the National Union is more elusive. It is involved in his attitude toward
the source and mode of political authority. He asserts the
practical dictum that the majority must govern. . . . Lincoln
was not a friend of the plebiscite or of the referendum; on the
contrary, he was a staunch believer in representative government in the strict sense. Why have the champions of stable
authority forgotten Lincoln's challenge to the country when refusing to yield to the clamor over military arrests? Asserting the
right of the President to assume in emergency vast authority, he
concludes that "if he uses the power justly, the . . . people
will probably justify him; if he abuses it, he is in their hands to
be dealt with by all the modes they have reserved to themselves
in the constitution." . . . What should hold one here is not Lincoln's wisdom, or lack of wisdom, but the boldness with which
he planted himself on the idea of delegated authority. He refused to be the mere spokesman of the people. He was in his
own mind their representative, on whom, for a time, certain
powers had been bestowed. For that time these powers were
his. . . .

There is a fourth main feature of Lincoln's conception. It
has been pointed out that most American reasoning about nationality is in terms of people. On this fact is grounded, I am
told, a distinction between the poetry inspired in America by
the World War and that of England. The American poets attach
their loyalty to the group of people, their countrymen. The
British poets, while having that, have also something more—a
sense of the soil, a loyalty to the very earth, our mother. Lincoln in his vision of nationality had outstripped his time and
had the British point of view.

"A nation," he asserts, "may be said to consist of its territory,
its people, and its laws. The territory is the only part that is of
certain durability. 'One generation passeth away and another
cometh, but the earth abideth forever.' It is of the first importance to duly consider and estimate this ever-enduring part." . . .

Lincoln's deepest significance was as a statesman of successful
democracy; incidental to this he was a statesman of nationalism,

laboring for cohesion in a people that were precipitating, as a chemist would say, the sense of nationality, but in whose general consciousness the precipitation was not complete.

24   *James A. Rawley*
The Nationalism of Abraham Lincoln

Lincoln's concept of American nationalism differed not only from the Southern interpretations he waged war to refute, but also from Northern interpretations in the formative years preceding his election as the nation's chief executive. His nationalism was a mid-century bridge between the earlier thought of the Founding Fathers, Henry Clay, and Daniel Webster, and the later thought of Francis Lieber and John W. Burgess. In his hierarchy of values he placed the nation uppermost—above peace, above abolition, above property rights, and even above the Constitution. . . .

Before he took the oath of office in 1861 Lincoln had developed a nationalism notable for its quiet fervor, its avoidance of spread-eagle expansionism, of strident Americanism, of cultural chauvinism, and of excessive legalism—differing markedly from the fervid sentiments of many mid-century nationalists. His pre-Presidential thought is best separated into its political, cultural, and economic components.

Lincoln's political nationalism stemmed from a belief in the uniqueness of the United States. Its government and society were an unexampled experiment—a successful experiment, indeed, but one which had yet to demonstrate its success to skeptical and less happy nations. What was the root of this distinctive national character? It was nothing less than a system of free

SOURCE. James A. Rawley, "The Nationalism of Abraham Lincoln," *Civil War History*, Vol. IX (1963), pp. 283–293. Reprinted by permission of the publisher and the author.

government. Here was the source of American political prosperity; without this living principle the state was worth nothing.

The incarnation of the spirit of American nationalism was for
him the Declaration of Independence. "I have often inquired of
myself," he reflected at Philadelphia in 1861,

"what great principle or idea it was that kept this confederacy
so long together. It was not the mere matter of the separation
of the colonies from the mother land; but something in that
Declaration giving liberty, not alone to the people of this country, but hope to the world for all time."

In this statement Lincoln put to one side many conventional
explanations of nationalism—language, common descent, cultural tradition, foreign perils, and historical territory—in favor
of an idea.

This central concept found legal embodiment in the Constitution—"the only safeguard of our liberties," as he put it. The
American government, held in restraint by the Constitution,
offered liberty and equality for all. "Free speech and discussion
and immunity from whip and tar and feathers, seem implied
by the guarantee to each state of a republican form of government," he deliberated. Through the public press our republican
institutions "can be best sustained by the diffusion of knowledge
and the due encouragement of a universal, national spirit of
inquiry and discussion of public events. . . ." He deemed religious and civil liberty "the noblest of causes," and found
American political institutions more conducive to their maintenance than any in human history.

Lincoln would not proscribe immigrants, would not make
them less eligible for the freedom of the Declaration than those
descended by blood from the Revolutionary fathers. ". . . They
have a right to claim it as though they were blood of the blood,
and flesh of the flesh of the men who wrote that Declaration . . . ," he insisted.

His conception of the place of the Negro in American society
flowed from his faith in the Declaration. Unlike Stephen A.
Douglas, he believed the Declaration embraced Negroes as well

as white persons, but that the commitment was to be realized in the future. Just as the Declaration did not decree immediate abolition of slavery, neither did its embodiment in the Constitution convert that document into an antislavery instrument, as Salmon P. Chase and Charles Sumner contended. The assertion that all men are created equal did not mean they were equal morally, intellectually, or physically, but that they were equal in certain inalienable rights. . . .

Lincoln's world-view was founded upon his belief in the impregnability, isolation, and pacific purposes of the United States. The world mission of America was to be an example, and little more. It was not to foment or assist revolutions abroad; it was not to liberate or to engage in missionary diplomacy. Rather, the United States would discharge its moral obligation by maintaining its example, by inspiring the hopes of man, by welcoming immigrants, and by sympathizing with those struggling to be free. The spirit animating the nation, he maintained, would eventually "grow and expand into the universal liberty of mankind."

A final element of his political nationalism was his espousal of the theoretical right of revolution. In a speech on the Mexican War, Congressman Lincoln had defended the right of the Mexicans and Texans in turn to revolt, recognizing the territorial authority of Texas, however, "just so far as she carried her revolution [geographically], by obtaining the *actual*, willing or unwilling, submission of the people. . . ." His "Resolutions in Behalf of Hungarian Freedom" had asserted "the right of any people, sufficiently numerous for national independence, to throw off, to revolutionize, their existing form of government. . . ." But he qualified his manifesto by a preamble emphasizing "our continued devotion to the principles of free institutions." The right of revolution he had been favoring was on behalf of human freedom, against Spain, Mexico, and Austria. Therefore it is not surprising to find Lincoln writing A. H. Stephens in January, 1859, that "The right of peaceable assembly and of petition, and by Article Fifth of the Constitution, the right of amendement, is the constitutional substitute [in this country] for revolution." The position he was to take as President he had declared well over two years before he assumed office.

The cultural aspects of Lincoln's pre-Presidential nationalism clustered about his emphasis upon the people rather than the state. Underlying this was his understanding of human nature. A persisting concept was his rejection of John Locke's famous notion of the malleability of human nature. ". . . Human nature cannot be changed," it is "God's decree," held Lincoln. Man was a blend of good and evil, and some men were better than others. Man was not good enough to live under a system of extreme individualism or anarchy; "if all men were just, there would still be *some,* though not so *much,* need of government." Men were moved by both high principle and self-interest. Part of Lincoln's case against slavery was that "it forces so many really good men amongst ourselves into open war with the very fundamental principles of civil liberty. . . ." Yet the good in man might be expected to prevail. Repeal the Missouri Compromise, repeal all past history, "you still cannot repeal human nature. It still will be the abundance of man's heart, that slavery extension is wrong. . . ."

The laboring element in the population elicited Lincoln's special sympathies. His famous statement that labor is prior to and independent of capital has often been quoted, sometimes to suggest a Marxian outlook, sometimes to suggest a defense of trade unionism. Actually, of course, it was neither; rather, it was a celebration of the virtues of an open society wherein a free laborer could rise to become a capitalist. His conception of labor looked to social harmony in place of strife, and herein he was more sanguine than his contemporary John Calhoun and possibly even Daniel Webster. . . .

It was the people who sustained the government and not the government the people. ". . . The strongest bulwark of any government . . . is the attachment of the people," he wrote. They would suffer much for its sake, but at some point danger might always be expected. "How shall we fortify against it?" he asked in an address in 1838. With an uncharacteristic outburst of chauvinism he urged indoctrination of loyalty. "Let reverence for the laws be breathed by every American mother, to the lisping babe, that prattles on her lap; let it be taught in schools, in seminaries, and in colleges. . . . in short, let it become the *political religion* of the nation. . . ." This exhortation might sound like a recipe for twentieth century totalitarianism were it not checked by counsel for proper repeal of bad laws. The people's loyalty was a staple of nationalism. In the crisis of the 1850's it was helping prevent dissolution of the Union. "You ought rather to appreciate how much the great body of the Northern people do crucify their feelings," he wrote his friend Joshua F. Speed in 1855, "in order to maintain their loyalty to the constitution and the Union."

Lincoln deemed territorial acquisition to be constitutional, and, while not advocating it, he did not oppose "honest acquisition." But he strenuously resisted grabs for territory that would aggravate the slavery question—"the one great disturbing element in our national politics." Finally, he showed little or no interest in the literary nationalism that colored American letters in his day, and indeed once admitted he had never finished reading a novel.

Lincoln's economic nationalism was an inheritance from Henry Clay, a general view of the capacity of the national government to promote the general welfare. In his first reputed public speech he admitted simply that "I am in favor of a national bank." On other occasions he defended the bank's constitutionality and advantages and criticized the Democrats' substitute—the subtreasury system. In his early years he aligned himself with Clay's nationalist policy on the protective tariff as "indispensably necessary to the prosperity of the American people," but by 1860–1861 was confessing that he had no "thoroughly matured judgment" on protectionism. His stand on internal improvements favored government support, though he did not countenance borrowing money or overexpansion of local projects. He sided with the nationalist principle of opening the public lands to free settlement, "so that every poor man may have a home."

Such measures implied a philosophy of broad construction of the Constitution looking to government intervention in the

economy to increase national wealth and promote human welfare. Beset by other issues during the war, however, Lincoln
as President did not much concern himself about economic
legislation.

When Abraham Lincoln became President of the United States
on March 4, 1861, he stood at a different stage in the development of nationalism than did his European statesman contemporaries Cavour and Bismarck. It was Lincoln's task not to
create a nation but to maintain one. His effort did not hinge,
fundamentally, on power rivalries of foreign nations but on pre-
plexing internal dissensions among states with a long history of
political cooperation. His task was eased by an American consensus on certain fundamentals, but complicated by a fierce
conflict over constitutional interpretation and the place of
slavery in the national polity. The contours of his task were
rounded out by three generations of discord over these issues
and by the secession of seven states even before he was clothed
with power.

Lincoln gave his own definition of a nation in 1862: "A
nation may be said to consist of its territory, its people, and
its laws." The element of territory was commonly stressed by
European theorists of nationalism, who found in the concept
of a historical homeland and agrarianism, powerful springs of
national sentiment. Though Lincoln had paid little notice to
territory as an element of American nationalism before 1861,
in the First Inaugural he stressed the unity imposed upon the
American people by their common territory. "Physically speaking, we cannot separate," he maintained. War would not settle
questions of intercourse, and separation would only aggravate
disputes over fugitive slaves and the foreign slave trade. He
spoke of "this favored land," and in closing referred movingly
to "The mystic chords of memory, stretching from every battlefield, and patriot grave, to every living heart and hearthstone,
all over this broad land. . . ."

The enduring unity given Americans by the "national homestead" occupied a good deal of his State of the Union message
in 1862. The territory of the United States was well adapted
for "one national family" and not two or more. "Its vast extent,
and its variety of climate and productions, are of advantage,

in this age, for one people. . . . Steam, telegraphs, and intelligence, have brought these, to be an advantageous combination for one people."

He turned next to a close analysis of American topography. There was no suitable line for separation. The boundary between free and slave states consisted for one-third its length of rivers easily crossed; the remaining segment was nothing more than a surveyor's line across which people might walk. Separation could not be achieved by scratching demarcations on parchment.

The great interior region between the Alleghenies and the Rockies, and north of the line where corn and cotton cultures met, posed special difficulties. In Lincoln's estimate, this was the great elongated nucleus of the republic; the other parts were but marginal to it. It was destined to have an immense population, and in the production of material subsistence it was one of the most important regions of the world. But it had no seacoast. Separation of the Union would cut it off from its trade outlets to Europe, South America, Africa, and Asia. Divide the nation between North and South however one might, there could be no commerce between separated sections "except on terms dictated by" a foreign government. Lincoln did not argue the advantages of territorial unity to Northern merchants or to the Northern people, but characteristically urged the South to recognize the folly of breaking a natural customs union advantageous to all Americans.

The national homestead, Lincoln concluded, was a permanent mandate for unity. Sectional contention, therefore, did not spring from territorial differences, but from only transient causes. "Our strife pertains to ourselves," he argued, ". . . and it can, without convulsion, be hushed forever with the passing of one generation." . . .

The second element in Lincoln's wartime definition of a nation was people. "This country, with its institutions, belongs to the people who inhabit it." They were the same people North and South; the nation belonged to all.

The war seems to have reinforced his faith in the public—"this great tribunal." Free institutions had developed the powers and improved the condition of "our whole people, beyond any example in the world." From almost every military regiment could be chosen "a president, a cabinet, a congress, and perhaps a court, abundantly competent to administer the government itself." The plenteous outpouring of loyalty in April, 1861, had shown him that "the people will save their government, if the government itself, will do its part, only indifferently well." The war was not a conflict of militarists, politicians, or classes; it was essentially a people's contest, "a war upon the first principles of popular government—the rights of the people." The people's stake in the war—maintaining a nation whose leading object was to elevate the condition of men—was well understood by the public, he felt.

Uppermost was his faith that "workingmen are the basis of all governments." In a letter of 1864 he made clear his conception of free labor in an open society. Laboring men of the world should unite by a bond of sympathy only less strong than the family tie. They should beware of the divisive force of prejudice and hostility. But labor solidarity should not lead to a war on property. "Property is the fruit of labor—property is desirable—is a positive good in the world. That some should be rich, shows that others may become rich, and hence is just encouragement to industry and enterprise." He therefore advocated social harmony and defined opportunity for social mobility in terms of the individual rather than the class. He once used himself as an example. To the assembled 166th Ohio Regiment he declared, "I happen temporarily to occupy this big White House. I am a living witness that any one of your children may look to come here as my father's child has."

Under popular government, Lincoln observed, "The chief magistrate derives all his authority from the people. . . ." This fiduciary relationship between President and people, he believed, warranted his exercise of extra-Constitutional authority in the national emergency. Presidential actions not explicitly authorized by the people might be made in their interest. If the President "uses the power justly, the . . . people will probably justify him; if he abuses it, he is in their hands to be dealt with by all the modes they have reserved to themselves in the Constitution."

One of these modes was the Presidential election, which occurred in normal course once during the war. It added not a little to the strain, admitted Lincoln, for "It has long been a grave question whether any government not *too* strong for the liberties of its people, can be strong enough to maintain its own existence, in great emergencies." So viewed, the outcome of the 1864 election was a success; moreover, it demonstrated the people's determination to preserve the Union. "The most reliable indication of public purpose in this country," he remarked approvingly, "is derived through our popular elections."

Popular sovereignty went hand in hand with majority rule. In his First Inaugural, Lincoln . . . observed that over slavery the American people divided into a majority and minority. "If the minority will not acquiesce, the majority must, or the government must cease." He applied this doctrine of popular sovereignty not merely to mooted questions where the Constitution was silent, but also to certain kinds of decisions already made by the Supreme Court, having in mind the proslavery Dred Scott case: ". . . If the whole policy of the government, upon vital questions affecting the whole people, is to be irrevocably fixed by decisions of the Supreme Court, the instant they are made, in ordinary litigation between parties, in personal actions, the people will have ceased, to be their own rulers. . . ."

The people's loyalty to the nation was Lincoln's reliance. Skillfully he appealed to it, even exploited it, through his wartime messages to Congress and letters (often ostensibly private but intended for the public). In these documents he put his case, the national case, with glowing words and persuasive logic; among the best examples of his letters are those to Horace Greeley, Erastus Corning, J. C. Conkling, and Mrs. Bixby. The two Inaugurals and the Gettysburg Address are classics, in part because of the national vision limned in them and the inspiring faith in "government of the people, by the people, for the people. . . ." A good portion of the First Inaugural is addressed to those "who really love the Union. . . ."

His conception of loyalty embraced the use of oaths, but the oaths were to be liberal—for insuring future allegiance only—and no man was to be forced to take one. His amnesty proclamation of December, 1863, embodied an oath that he looked upon as a means of waging war, hastening peace, and effecting reunion. It would encourage desertion from the Confederacy, assure certain rights to the oath taker, and form a nucleus of loyal citizens who, he thought, would give an affirmative answer to the question he put in his last public address: "Can Louisiana be brought into proper practical relation with the Union *sooner* by *sustaining* . . . her new state government?" And what would be true of Louisiana would be true of other seceded states. . . .

The third essential point of Lincoln's final concept of a nation was its laws: fundamental or higher law, organic or constitutional law, and statutory or legislative law. The American nation was founded upon law; it emanated from the fundamental law, and proceeded through organic law to statutory law.

This orderly progession lay at the heart of his conception of the origin of the nation. For nearly three generations the philosophical nature of the Union had been hotly contested. Among the most influential views was John C. Calhoun's theory that the Union was merely a compact among sovereign states, which had created it by writing and ratifying the Constitution. Each state might nullify an act of the national legislature by following a formula patterned on the mode of ratification. Indeed, each state might withdraw unilaterally from the Union by following a prescribed plan.

Various challenges to national sovereignty had previously been repudiated by John Marshall, Andrew Jackson, and Daniel Webster. Not until 1860, however, had any state exercised an asserted right of secession. To the question of the origin of the nation Lincoln addressed himself in his First Inaugural and elsewhere. He contended that the nation was *not* the creation of the Constitutional Convention and the state ratifying conventions, was *not* born in 1787–1788, and was *not* a compact among the states. He argued that the nation was older than the Constitution, and even older than the states. It was born in 1774, founded by the Articles of Association (or perhaps in 1776, as he suggested in the Gettysburg Address). The birth of the nation before the colonies became states gave the nation precedence over the states; "The original ones passed into the Union even *before* they cast off their British colonial dependence. . . ." Formed by the Articles of Association, the American nation

"was matured and continued by the Declaration of Independence in 1776. It was further matured and the faith of all the then thirteen states expressedly plighted and engaged that it should be perpetual by the Articles of Confederation in 1778. And finally, in 1787, one of the declared objects for ordaining and establishing the Constitution was *to form a more perfect union.*"

Calhoun's starting point, therefore, was actually the outcome of an organic progress.

In his conception of the nation as a living organism, capable of evolutionary growth, Lincoln differed not merely from Calhoun but also from those nationalist stalwarts Marshall, Jackson, and Webster. Marshall in *McCulloch* v. *Maryland,* for example, like Calhoun saw the origin of the nation in the Constitution. He read its history differently, however, insisting that the Constitution derived its whole authority not from the states but from the people. Jackson, in his "Proclamation to the People of South Carolina," shared Calhoun's assumptions that the nation originated with the Constitution and that the nation was a compact. But it was a compact to form a government that "operates directly on the people individually, not upon the States"; and "it is precisely because it is a compact that" the states could not breach it. Webster, too, as in his Second Reply to Hayne, agreed that the nation began with the constitutional contract. However, it was "an executed contract" and he roundly denied that the national government was the creature or agent of the states. "It is, Sir, the people's Constitution, the people's government, made for the people, and answerable to the people."

Lincoln, then, departed from the consensus that the American nation was born with the Constitution and that it was a contract. He was perhaps the first President to emphasize strongly the

ideas that the Union was more than a government and that the
American political organization was a nation-state. He reached
beyond the Constitution to the mystique of "its territory, its
people, and its laws."

25   *K. C. Wheare*
Lincoln's Devotion to the Union, Intense and Supreme

Lincoln's devotion to the Union is, in its intensity and supremacy, almost startling. He was prepared to go much farther
to prevent the break-up of the Union than ever he proposed to
go to prevent the extension of slavery. Yet he is usually
thought of primarily as the liberator of slaves and the great
enemy of slavery. He had said himself that slavery was a wrong
and that its extension in the Territories of the United States
should be resisted. But he never said that it should be resisted
by the secession of the North from the Union or by the ex-
pulsion of the South from the Union, and above all he never
said that it should be resisted by force of arms. He was ready
to see the slavery question settled by vote and to abide by the
result, and this, too, although he felt sure that the result would
be that the United States became all slave or all free. But none
the less he held that whether the Union be a free Union or a
slave Union, he was determined that he must preserve the Union.
And when he came in the course of the war to proclaim the
emancipation of slaves, he did so as a measure to help preserve
the Union; it was a measure of military necessity. Abraham
Lincoln went to war, not to prevent or abolish slavery, but to
preserve the Union of which he had been elected head.

SOURCE. Reprinted with permission of The Macmillan Company, The
English Universities Press Limited and the author from *Abraham Lincoln
and the United States* by K. C. Wheare, pp. 158–160, 162–166, 168–175. First
printed in 1948. First Collier Edition 1966.

There is much in Lincoln's attitude here that is puzzling. His attitude to slavery is perhaps not so puzzling as his attitude to the Union. After all, as will have been appreciated from the account given so far, Lincoln's attitude on slavery was consistent all through his political life. He opposed its extension in the Territories, but he opposed also interference with slavery in the states; and whenever he considered abolition, it was gradual and with compensation. He was on the slavery issue a moderate, not an abolitionist and not an extensionist. Yet, if this were so, when the states of the lower South seceded, why not let them go? They were slave states; Lincoln did not advocate interfering with slavery in them; outside the Union they could have no influence upon Union policy, no influence upon the Territories. Surely it would have been better, from the point of view of preventing the extension of slavery, to let them go? That was what some people in the North advocated. In January 1861, before Lincoln's inauguration, Horace Greeley used the phrase: "Wayward sisters, depart in peace." And, who knows, had they gone, might they not, after a decade or so, have abolished slavery, and have been ready to return to the Union? To none of these arguments was Lincoln prepared to assent. The Union must be preserved. There could be no half-measures here. . . .

How did Lincoln justify his supreme devotion to the Union? First of all, he believed that secession was illegal; it was contrary to the terms of the Constitution of the United States. In his First Inaugural he said: "I hold, that in contemplation of universal law and of the Constitution, the Union of these states is perpetual." The legality of secession was a subject of intense dispute in the days of the Civil War and afterwards. It was not only the South which believed in the legality of secession. There were men both in North and South who were Unionists at the time of Lincoln's election, but who none the less believed in the legality of secession, although they did not favour its exercise in this particular case. The most careful exposition of the legality of secession was found indeed in the writings of Alexander H. Stephens, who . . . favoured the maintenance of the Union and advised his own state, Georgia, not to secede.

When secession was decided upon, he went with his state and became Vice-President of the Confederacy.

Was Lincoln's view of the Constitution correct? If the Constitution itself is considered as an isolated document, there is no doubt that it contains no provision, express or implied, conferring a unilateral right of secession upon any state, whether upon the government of the state or the people of the state. It was true that the Tenth Amendment to the Constitution, passed in 1791, gave some support to the contention of the secessionists. It ran: "The powers not delegated to the United States by the Constitution, nor prohibited by it to the states, are reserved to the states respectively, or to the people." It now became a matter of argument what powers had been delegated to the United States. The argument of the secessionists was that, whatever powers had been delegated, the states—and by the states they meant the people of the states, not the governments—had retained their sovereignty and were thus fully empowered, if they thought fit, to withdraw from the Union. The Tenth Amendment, in the opinion of Jefferson Davis, for example, as stated in his First Message to the Confederate Congress, had placed "beyond any pretence of doubt the reservation by the states of all their sovereign rights and powers not expressly delegated to the United States by the Constitution."

So there arose the question whether or not "sovereignty" had actually been surrendered by the states. The discussion of this question soon involved an historical argument. What had the framers of the Constitution themselves believed that they had done? Did they think that they had created a sovereign government over the states, or did they believe that they had left sovereignty entirely with the states? On this broader historical argument it is necessary to say that there was a good case on both sides. The Fathers of the Constitution had not all thought the same thing and some of them had not spoken unambiguously. Lincoln had a case; so had Jefferson Davis and Stephens. And of the two, it must be said that Lincoln overstated his case. He said in his First Inaugural: "The Union is much older than the Constitution. It was formed, in fact, by the Articles of Association in 1774. It was matured and continued by the Declaration of Independence in 1776. It was further matured and the faith of all the then thirteen states expressly plighted and engaged that it should be perpetual, by the Articles of Confederation in 1778. And finally, in 1787, one of the declared objects for ordaining and establishing the Constitution was 'to form a more perfect Union.' " In fact, although some form of association between the states was older than the Constitution, those forms of association were different from the Union. The Union which existed in 1861 was produced by the Constitution. To say that it was older was to fall back on an historical error.

Taking Lincoln's case moderately, however, and putting it beside the secessionist case, it is not easy to say by a reference to the opinions of the Fathers of the Constitution which was the true interpretation. But the contest in 1861 was carried on in extreme terms. The secessionists claimed full sovereignty for the states; their opponents claimed full sovereignty for the Union. What the Constitution of the United States actually did was to divide sovereignty between the Union and the states. It created a government for the Union, not a mere agent of the states; it left governments for the states, not mere subordinate administrative agencies. But the contestants of 1861 could not speak in terms of divided sovereignty. The political conceptions of an absolutist theory of sovereignty were still accepted. It was only after the Civil War, when the doctrine of the right of secession was defeated by force of arms, that its historical and logical foundations became discredited. The South had a case which was strong in past history, but it proved to have no future. . . .

One result of the victory of the North in the Civil War was that the view of the Union as indestructible came to prevail. It received official sanction from the Supreme Court in 1868 in the case of *Texas v. White*. . . .

But the dispute between Lincoln and the seceders was not merely a legal dispute. Both sides were anxious, it is true, to prove that their actions were legal. But they believed also that they were morally justified in the action they took, and they were supported throughout in their conflict by the sense of moral rightness. Here one leaves the ground of a legal right of secession and moves to the ground of a moral right of rebellion or revolution. Abraham Lincoln could not deny, in the light of his country's history, that there were circumstances in which, in the words of the American Declaration of Independence in 1776, "it becomes necessary for one people to dissolve the political bonds which have connected them with another." He admitted the existence of the moral right to rebel. But he asserted that in 1860 and 1861 the seceding states had no adequate justification for exercising this right. And he gave several reasons for so thinking.

First of all, he said that secession did not provide the remedy for the grievances which the South professed to have. For what was the dispute? "One section of our country believes slavery is right, and ought to be extended, while the other believes it it wrong, and ought not to be extended." How can secession solve this problem? It makes the extension of slavery impossible, so that the South gains nothing there. It makes it harder, not easier, to deal with questions like fugitive slaves and tariffs. Yet these questions are bound to arise, for the two unions will be side by side. "The foreign slave trade, now imperfectly suppressed, would be ultimately revived, without restriction, in one section, while fugitive slaves, now only partially surrendered, would not be surrendered at all by the other. . . . Suppose you go to war, you cannot fight always; and when, after much loss on both sides, and no gain on either, you cease fighting, the identical old questions as to terms of intercourse are again upon you." These words were used in his First Inaugural. The argument was developed in more detail in his Annual Message to Congress in December 1862. Secession is ineffectual as a means of settling the disputes. It will achieve nothing except to break up the Union. It achieves a wrong and it sets nothing right.

And this leads Lincoln to his next argument. He believes not only that secession is morally unjustified because it will do no good; he believes also that it will do positive harm. It will be a blow to democratic and free government all over the world. It will make people believe that democratic government lacks the qualities necessary for good and effective government.

In his First Message to Congress, in their special session, July 4, 1861, he used these words:

"This issue embraces more than the fate of these United States. It presents to the whole family of man the question whether a constitutional republic or democracy—a government of the people by the same people—can or cannot maintain its territorial integrity against its own domestic foes. It presents the question whether discontented individuals, too few in numbers to control administration according to organic law in any case, can always, upon the pretences made in this case or any other pretences, or arbitrarily without any pretence, break up their government and thus practically put an end to free government upon the earth. It forces us to ask: 'Is there, in all republics, this inherent and fatal weakness?' 'Must a government, of necessity, be too strong for the liberties of its own people, or too weak to maintain its own existence?' "

And it was this same idea he had in mind when he said, in the famous remarks at Gettysburg on November 19, 1863, that the Civil War was testing whether a nation "conceived in liberty and dedicated to the proposition that all men are created equal" could long endure; that the object of the war was to ensure "that government of the people, by the people, and for the people, shall not perish from the earth." Lincoln opposed secession because it struck a blow at democratic government.

Yet it is natural to ask, has a minority no right of rebellion in a democratic government? More particularly, if by democratic government is meant the rule of the majority, may there not be occasions when the majority is tyrannical or where the division of opinion between majority and minority is so acute, that the minority is entitled to leave? It is not certain what Lincoln's answer would be to a very general question of this sort. It is likely that he would admit that there could be circumstances in which a minority would be justified in rebelling against a majority. But in a true democracy, as he conceived it, where all sides had the right freely to advocate their view, the minority must acquiesce in the proposition of majority rule. More particularly was the South obliged to acquiesce when its right to perpetuate slavery in its own borders was conceded by the majority. Lincoln's argument seems to be that, although the majority may not always be right, the consequences of rejecting majority rule are so serious—they produce anarchy—that it is better to follow the majority than to rebel.

In his First Inaugural he said: "Plainly, the central idea of secession is the essence of anarchy. A majority held in restraint by constitutional checks and limitations, and always changing easily with deliberate changes of popular opinions and sentiments, is the only true sovereign of a free people. Whoever rejects it does, of necessity, fly to anarchy or to despotism. Unanimity is impossible; the rule of a minority, as a permanent arrangement, is wholly inadmissible; so that, rejecting the majority principle, anarchy or despotism in some form is all that is left." It was therefore justifiable in a democracy, when its central principle was attacked, to put down by force those who resisted it. This was the substance of a passage in the message to Congress at its special session in 1861:

"Our popular government has often been called an experiment. Two points in it our people have already settled—the successful establishing and the successful administering of it. One still remains—its successful maintenance against a formidable internal attempt to overthrow it. It is now for them to demonstrate to the world that those who can fairly carry on election can also suppress a rebellion: that ballots are the rightful and peaceful successors of bullets; and that when ballots have fairly and constitutionally decided, there can be no successful appeal back to bullets; that there can be no successful appeal, except to ballots themselves, at succeeding elections. Such will be a great lesson of peace; teaching men that what they cannot take by an election, neither can they take by a war, teaching all the folly of being the beginners of a war."

This is a hard saying for a permanent minority. It means that they must acquiesce perpetually in a line of political action of which they disapprove. Majority rule and the ballot box hold out hope to a minority that has some likelihood of becoming itself a majority one day. But for the South there seemed no such likelihood. Be the government as democratic as it possibly could be, with every safeguard of free speech, the slave states were now in a minority and they could never become a majority. Their way of life, their social organisation, could not prevail; on the contrary, they might well suffer in the Union. What comfort was there for them in recourse to the ballot box? What chance for them in a system of majorities "always changing easily with deliberate changes of popular opinions and sentiments?" That was the position of the South. Yet it seems clear that Lincoln held fast to the view that, permanent minority as they were, they must acquiesce in the views of the majority. To do otherwise would be wrong, for it would destroy government.

It is startling to realise that Lincoln did not believe in the principle of self-determination of peoples. The South claimed themselves to be a distinct people; they strove for independence as the Irish strove to free themselves from the United Kingdom. Yet Lincoln fought against them with more determination than any British Prime Minister fought against Ireland in the nineteenth and twentieth centuries. . . .

To those who associate the principle of self-determination with the United States it comes as something of a shock to find that Abraham Lincoln, associated in one's mind with liberty and democracy, should argue so firmly against it. Yet the fact is unavoidable. Woodrow Wilson, the greatest President of the United States between Lincoln and Franklin Roosevelt, advocated the principle of self-determination for the settlement of national-minority problems in Europe. He was not a blind and absolute believer in the efficiency of the principle, nor, we may assert, was Lincoln a blind and absolute opponent of it. But Woodrow Wilson may be said to have given pre-eminence to self-determination, to secession and to disintegration as agents for good government; Lincoln gave pre-eminence to majority rule, to union and integration.

SUGGESTIONS FOR ADDITIONAL READING

Lincoln literature is not only extensive in itself but also very difficult to separate from the enormous mass of writing on the Civil War. What follows is a highly selective list of books and essays useful for further exploration of the problems treated in this volume. Excellent bibliograpies will be found in J. G. Randall and David Donald, *The Civil War and Reconstruction* (Boston, 1961); and in the second and fourth volumes of J. G. Randall, *Lincoln the President* (4 vols.; New York, 1945–1955; volume IV completed by Richard N. Current). Two essays on the growth of Lincoln literature are David M. Potter, "The Lincoln Theme and American National Historiography," in his *The South and the Sectional Conflict* (Baton Rouge, 1968); and Don E. Fehrenbacher, *The Changing Image of Lincoln in American Historiography* (pamphlet; Oxford, England, 1968).

The definitive edition of Lincoln's writings is Roy P. Basler, ed., *The Collected Works of Abraham Lincoln* (9 vols.; New Brunswick, N. J., 1953–1955). Archer H. Shaw, ed., *The Lincoln Encyclopedia* (New York, 1950), is a topically arranged compilation of Lincoln's words, but it contains some spurious items. For Lincoln's incoming correspondence, one must turn to the Robert Todd Lincoln Collection in the Manuscripts Division of the Library of Congress, microfilm copies of which are now held by a number of libraries.

The Randall and Donald work cited above is the standard text on the Civil War era. Preeminent among general studies is Allan Nevins' great but unfinished work covering the years 1847–1863: *Ordeal of the Union* (2 vols.; New York, 1947); *The Emergence of Lincoln* (2 vols.; New York, 1950); *The War for the Union* (2 vols. to date; New York, 1959–1960). Bruce Catton, *The Centennial History of the Civil War•* (3 vols.; Garden City, N. Y.) is authoritative and eminently readable. Some passages in Robert Penn Warren's little book, *The Legacy of the*

Civil War (New York, 1961) are among the wisest comments ever written on the nature of Lincoln's leadership.

The best one-volume biography is Benjamin P. Thomas, *Abraham Lincoln* (New York, 1952). Less successful, but still very useful, is Reinhard H. Luthin, *The Real Abraham Lincoln* (Englewood Cliffs, N. J., 1960). Two older biographies remain worth reading: William H. Herndon and Jesse W. Weik, *Herndon's Lincoln: The True Story of a Great Life* (3 vols.; Chicago, 1889); and Lord Charnwood, *Abraham Lincoln* (New York, 1917). Herndon's personal portrait of his law partner, an invaluable but unreliable source, is best read in the one-volume version edited and annotated by Paul M. Angle (Greenwich, Conn., 1961). Charnwood's book, though dated, is notable for its thoughtful views on the universal significance of Lincoln's career. The two outstanding multivolume biographies are Randall's scholarly *Lincoln the President*, cited above, and Carl Sandburg's monumental work, *Abraham Lincoln: The Prairie Years* (2 vols.; New York, 1926), and *Abraham Lincoln: The War Years* (4 vols.; New York, 1939). Richard N. Current, *The Lincoln Nobody Knows* (New York, 1958), is a unique, topically arranged treatment of those aspects of Lincoln's career that have inspired the most scholarly controversy.

Much can be learned about Lincoln from biographies of men closely associated with him: David Donald, *Lincoln's Herndon* (New York, 1948); Willard L. King, *Lincoln's Manager, David Davis* (Cambridge, Mass., 1960); George Fort Milton, *The Eve of Conflict: Stephen A. Douglas and the Needless War* (Boston, 1934); Maurice Baxter, *Orville H. Browning* (Bloomington, Ind., 1957); Glyndon G. Van Deusen, *William Henry Seward* (New York, 1967); Benjamin P. Thomas and Harold M. Hyman, *Stanton* (New York, 1962); Marvin R. Cain, *Lincoln's Attorney General, Edward Bates of Missouri* (Columbia, Mo., 1965); Stephen E. Ambrose, *Halleck* (Baton Rouge, 1962); Warren W. Hassler, Jr., *General George B. McClellan* (Baton Rouge, 1957); and many others.

Any thorough study of Lincoln's leadership must give some attention to his prepresidential career. The most useful works for this purpose are: Albert J. Beveridge, *Abraham Lincoln, 1809–1858* (2 vols.; Boston, 1928); Donald W. Riddle, *Congressman Abraham Lincoln* (Urbana, Ill., 1957); Richard Hofstadter, "Abraham Lincoln and the Self-Made Myth," in his *The American Political Tradition* (New York, 1948); Don E. Fehrenbacher, *Prelude to Greatness: Lincoln in the 1850's* (Stanford, 1962); Richard A. Heckman, *Lincoln vs. Douglas: The Great Debates Campaign* (Washington, 1967); William Baringer,

Lincoln's Rise to Power (Boston, 1937); and Reinhard H. Luthin, *The First Lincoln Campaign* (Cambridge, Mass., 1944). Harry V. Jaffa, *Crisis of the House Divided* (New York, 1959), is a learned and original study of Lincoln's political thought, with special reference to the issues in his debates with Douglas.

On the secession crisis and Fort Sumter, there are three excellent studies by leading historians: David M. Potter, *Lincoln and His Party in the Secession Crisis* (New Haven, 1942; paperback edition with important new preface, 1962); Kenneth M. Stampp, *And the War Came* (Baton Rouge, 1950); and Richard N. Current, *Lincoln and the First Shot* (Philadelphia, 1963). See also Potter's essay, "Why the Republicans Rejected Both Compromise and Secession," together with comment by Stampp, in George Harmon Knoles, ed., *The Crisis of the Union* (Baton Rouge, 1965). Two popular accounts of the Fort Sumter affair are W. A. Swanberg, *First Blood* (New York, 1958); and Roy Meredith, *Storm Over Sumter* (New York, 1957). Lincoln is blamed for the outbreak of hostilities in Charles W. Ramsdell, "Lincoln and Fort Sumter," *Journal of Southern History*, III (1937), 259–288; and with less restraint in John S. Tilley, *Lincoln Takes Command* (Chapel Hill, 1941). J. G. Randall, "Lincoln's Sumter Dilemma," in his *Lincoln, the Liberal Statesman* (New York, 1947), is in part a rebuttal to the Ramsdell article. Richard N. Current, "The Confederates and the First Shot," *Civil War History*, VII (1961), 357–369, is an interesting inversion of the Ramsdell thesis.

The two principal studies of Lincoln's military leadership are both decidedly favorable: T. Harry Williams, *Lincoln and His Generals* (New York, 1952); and Colin R. Ballard, *The Military Genius of Abraham Lincoln* (London, 1926). See also Williams' essay, "The Military Leadership of North and South," in David Donald, ed., *Why the North Won the Civil War* (Baton Rouge, 1960). The ranking history of the Army of the Potomac is Bruce Catton's trilogy, *Mr. Lincoln's Army; Glory Road;* and *A Stillness at Appomattox* (Garden City, N. Y., 1951–1953). Exhaustive and opinionated is Kenneth P. Williams, *Lincoln Finds a General* (5 vols.; New York, 1949–1959). Robert V. Bruce, *Lincoln and the Tools of War* (Indianapolis, 1956), demonstrates Lincoln's keen interest in the development of military technology.

There is no comprehensive study of Lincoln's political leadership. Some of the most perceptive writing on the subject is in David Donald, *Lincoln Reconsidered* (2nd ed.; New York, 1961); and in Norman

A. Graebner, ed., *The Enduring Lincoln* (Urbana, Ill., 1959). Three important specialized studies are Harry J. Carman and Reinhard H. Luthin, *Lincoln and the Patronage* (New York, 1943); William B. Hesseltine, *Lincoln and the War Governors* (New York, 1948); and William F. Zornow, *Lincoln and the Party Divided* (Norman, Okla., 1954), which deals with the election of 1864. T. Harry Williams, *Lincoln and the Radicals* (Madison, Wis., 1941), is hostile to the Radicals and emphasizes their conflict with Lincoln. Hans L. Trefousse takes the contrary view, as his subtitle indicates in *The Radical Republicans, Lincoln's Vanguard for Racial Justice* (New York, 1969). William D. Mallam treats a neglected aspect of the subject in "Lincoln and the Conservatives," *Journal of Southern History,* XXVIII (1962), 31–45.

Benjamin Quarles, *Lincoln and the Negro* (New York, 1962); and John Hope Franklin, *The Emancipation Proclamation* (New York, 1963), are the standard scholarly works on those subjects. Excellent for the general background is James M. McPherson, *The Struggle for Equality: Abolitionists and the Negro in the Civil War and Reconstruction* (Princeton, 1964). Lincoln's attitude toward the Negro is debated with some heat in Ludwell H. Johnson, "Lincoln and Equal Rights: The Authenticity of the Wadsworth Letter," *Journal of Southern History,* XXXII (1966), 83–87; Harold M. Hyman, "Lincoln and Equal Rights for Negroes: The Irrelevancy of the Wadsworth Letter," *Civil War History,* XII (1966), 258–266; and Johnson, "Lincoln and Equal Rights: A Reply," ibid., XIII (1967), 66–73. Two articles examining Lincoln's interest in colonization of Negroes abroad are Warren A. Beck, "Lincoln and Negro Colonization in Central America," *Abraham Lincoln Quarterly,* VI (1950), 162–183; and Paul J. Scheips, "Lincoln and the Chiriqui Colonization Project," *Journal of Negro History,* XXXVII (1952), 418–453. For the enlistment of Negroes in the Union Army, see Dudley T. Cornish, *The Sable Arm* (New York, 1956).

A systematic study of Lincoln's thought on the Union and secession remains to be written. The following essays are helpful, however: Thomas J. Pressly, "Bullets and Ballots: Lincoln and the 'Right of Revolution,'" *American Historical Review,* LVII (1962), 647–662; Edmund Wilson, "Abraham Lincoln," in his *Patriotic Gore* (New York, 1962); and the introductory essay in Richard N. Current, ed., *The Political Thought of Abraham Lincoln* (Indianapolis, 1967). The best study of the reconstruction issue during Lincoln's presidency is Herman

Belz, *Reconstructing the Union* (Ithaca, N. Y., 1969). William B. Hesseltine, *Lincoln's Plan of Reconstruction* (Tuscaloosa, Ala., 1960), is much briefer but valuable. See also Ludwell H. Johnson, "Lincoln's Solution to the Problem of Peace Terms, 1864–1865," *Journal of Southern History*, XXXIV (1968), 576–586.